WORKS OF HESIOD

AND THE HOMERIC HYMNS

WORKS OF
HESIOD
AND THE
HOMERIC HYMNS

◈

WORKS AND DAYS
THEOGONY
THE HOMERIC HYMNS
THE BATTLE OF THE FROGS AND THE MICE

◈

TRANSLATED BY

DARYL HINE

◈

THE UNIVERSITY OF CHICAGO PRESS

Chicago & London

The University of Chicago Press, Chicago 60637
The University of Chicago Press, Ltd., London
© 2005 by The University of Chicago
All rights reserved. Published 2005
Paperback edition 2007
Printed in the United States of America

14 13 12   4 5

ISBN: 0-226-32965-8 (cloth)
ISBN-13: 978-0-226-32966-6 (paper)
ISBN-10: 0-226-32966-6 (paper)

The Homeric Hymns and *The Battle of the Frogs and the Mice* were previously
published by Atheneum in 1972; some changes have been made in this edition.

Library of Congress Cataloging-in Publication Data

Hesiod.
  [Works. English]
  Works of Hesiod and the Homeric hymns / translated by Daryl Hine.
    p. cm.
  Includes bibliographical references and index.
  ISBN 0-266-32965-8 (alk. paper)
  1. Didactic poetry, Greek—Translations into English.   2. Religious
  poetry, Greek—Translations into English.   3. Hymns, Greek (Classical)—
  Translations into English.   4. Fables, Greek—Translations into English.
  5. Gods, Greek—Poetry 6. Farm life—Poetry.   7. Seasons—Poetry.
  I. Battle of the frogs and mice. English.   II. Homeric hymns. English.
  III. Hine, Daryl.   IV. Title.
PA4010.E5 2005
881′.01—dc22

                                        2004008778

What is, however, to me all that stuff about oak trees and stones?

CONTENTS

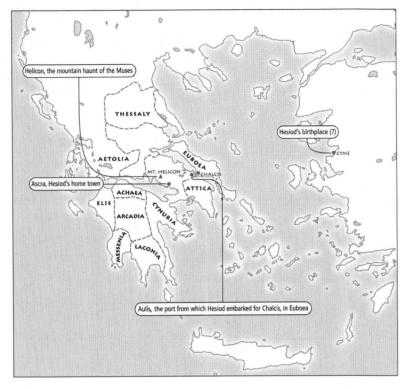

Helicon, the mountain haunt of the Muses

Hesiod's birthplace (?)

CYME

THESSALY

EUBOEA

AETOLIA

MT. HELICON
CHALCIS

Ascra, Hesiod's home town

ACHAEA
ATTICA

ELIS

ARCADIA
CYNURIA

MESSENIA
LACONIA

Aulis, the port from which Hesiod embarked for Chalcis, in Euboea

Greece, 800–700 BC

Greece, 600–500 BC

INTRODUCTION

Among the oldest known to us, these poems were, presumably, first recited and then written down, not to be read but to be listened to. This dictates their form, as verse, in this case dactylic hexameter: the stichic, or line-by-line, verse form as common to Greek and Latin epic as iambic pentameter is to English. Since a poem is not only its content but its form, this new translation attempts metrically to reproduce this long line in English, rather than, as some other translators have done, substituting our native equivalent, blank verse.

Though much scholarly ink has been squandered on the question of the relative antiquity of each of the poems, as well as of their respective, putative authors—whether, say, the *Theogony* preceded or postdated the *Works and Days*—suffice it to allege that both antedate any other extant poetry in Greek or any other European language. It should also be remembered that their age is not the most compelling aspect of these works.

In dealing with antiquity, ancient evidence, even when self-contradictory, is best; often it is all we have. Though it may seem nearsighted to expect those nearest the events in question to have the clearest view, their opinions, however ridiculous they may seem to an age more hampered by the rules of evidence, must bear a peculiar weight. The Roman emperor Hadrian (AD 76–138) sent to the Delphic oracle, the most respected and reliable in the classical world, to settle the debatable question as to the identity of the poet Homer, already legendary in Hadrian's day, and was vouchsafed this reply (in verse, as the Pythia always spoke the acknowledged metrical language of inspiration):

So you ask me about the unknown descent and the homeland
Of the ambrosial siren. Ithaca was his abode.
Just as Telemachus sired him, Epicaste the daughter of Nestor
Bore him and mothered him, most sophisticated of mortals.

If it would thus seem that the greatest of poets, often referred to simply as "the Poet," had devoted his most popular work to the exploits of his grandfather, this would be highly laudable by heroic standards. Though the answer is fabulous, there is little in Homer or Hesiod that is not. But the oracle, by a mantic example of *petitio principi,* or begging the question, has identified the author wholly and exclusively with his works. "Homer" is to be found only in the *Iliad,* the *Odyssey,* and the *Homeric Hymns,* where he is not named, and nowhere else. "Homer" is less a name, or a misnomer, than an epithet, meaning, according to one account, "blind" in an Aeolian dialect. The only autobiographical authorial reference in the Homeric corpus occurs in the *Hymn to Delian Apollo* (III):

"Who, do you think, is the man that is sweetest of singers, O maidens . . . ?"
"He is a blind man whose home is on Chios, that rugged and rockbound
Island, and all of his poems are excellent, now and hereafter."

But modern scholarship knows that there were many Homers, or Homeridae ("sons of Homer"), and we can never really know which composed what, nor do we really need to. The narrative structure of the *Odyssey* at least suggests to me a single, supreme compositional intelligence: it does not read like a poem written by a committee. But the oracle was, as usual, right; for "Homer" we have only to look in Homer. Otherwise we know even less of him than of Shakespeare, that other supremely reticent poet. It says something of fame that the most famous poets should also be the least known.

A Delphic oracle about Hesiod is also recorded, but as it concerns his death rather than his birth, it is less arresting. This and other information, or misinformation, are to be found in the undated *Contest of Homer and Hesiod,* a slanging match or cento which, in a perverse tribute to the taste of its time, Hesiod is said to have won. The question of the chronological as well as the aesthetic primacy of the two poets was debatable even then. If Hesiod seems sometimes to be quoting Homer, why should not this be read as Homer quoting Hesiod? The great Alexandrian critic Aristarchus objected to the second line of the *Odyssey* as having been stolen from Hesiod, though hardly a Hesiod we know. The similarities and differences between the two poets, or rather between their bodies of work, remind me of the relationship between Shakespeare and Marlowe—though, so far as I know, no one has put forward the thesis that Hesiod wrote the Homeric poems. A parallel exists in their historic proximity as well as in the vastly different quantity and quality of their work. Even the variously dated *Homeric Hymns* must strike any reader as superior, at least poetically, to most of Hesiod's output. A reader may not, however, immediately see why they should be called hymns or especially Homeric, if by that we mean (as we must) the style of the *Iliad* and the *Odyssey,* different as they are. Lays, rather, with brief invocations to the deity concerned, they are no more than short stories, abbreviated but well-plotted myths about some of the Olympian deities.

It is only toward the end of the *Theogony* (circa line 900 and following) that Hesiod deals with the Olympian pantheon so familiar from later classical poetry as well as the *Homeric Hymns.* The poem's material is all but purely traditional; the form Hesiod gave it was also the meter of the Homeric poems. But the organization, or disorganization, of the poem is attributable purely to the farmer-poet. The incidence of formulaic lines and phrases is, of course, due less to invention than to transmission, as a demonstrable and indispensable element in oral verse.

We shall never know who Homer was, but there can be no doubt about Hesiod's identity, although scholars may quibble over the authenticity of given passages in his poems. From his first encounter with the Muses on Mount Helicon, through his success in a poetry competition where the prize was an iron pot, to his quarrels with his brother Perses, his personal history exerts more appeal for the modern reader than do the fabulous histories of the gods. Yet in Hesiod's work we find the first occurrences of stories such as that of Prometheus the fire bringer, Pandora (whose box was really a jar), and the wars of the gods and the titans, stories echoed in other mythologies.

Hesiod knows no Homeric reticence and puts himself and his concerns front and center in his poems, sometimes, endearingly, even ahead of the gods. But unlike Homer, who takes his world as he found it, he also provides us with an account of the creation, and not only in the *Theogony* (The Genesis of the Gods).

The details of Hesiod's biographical origin are both specific and succinct:

Our father settled near Helicon Mount, in a miserable village,
Ascra: it's horrid in winter, obnoxious in summer, and never
Pleasant.

(*Works and Days*, 629–31)

Ascra is in Boeotia, which with its Doric dialect was considered notoriously rude and rustic, at least by the polished inhabitants of Attica. Much more interesting is Hesiod's moving, even magical account of his poetic vocation as directly dictated by the Muses:

Such are the goddesses who taught Hesiod beautiful songs once
While he was shepherding lambs in the shadow of Helicon's holy
Mountain, and these were the very first words they uttered to me, those
Nymphs of Olympus, the daughters of Zeus, who carries the aegis.
"Wilderness shepherds, ignoble excuses for men, merely bellies.
We are accustomed to tell many lies that resemble the facts, and
We are accustomed to speak, when we wish to, the literal truth, too."

So the articulate daughters of Zeus the magnificent spoke, and
Gave me a staff, a sprout they had plucked of the vigorous laurel:
It was a marvelous thing. They inspired me with vocal, prophetic
Song, to enunciate matters to come and others that have been.
Me they commanded to sing of the race of the blessed immortals,
Hymning themselves at beginning and end of every poem.
What is, however, to me all that stuff about oak trees and stones?

(*Theogony*, 21–34)

Those who see a disjunction between the Hesiod first named and the
first-person poet as his successor, finely discriminating between the
pseudonymous and the anonymous, may be pursuing a prehistoric fata
morgana or will-o'-the-wisp, misled by the poet's sudden veer from the
third to the first person for himself. It is doubtless to this passage that we
owe our identification of the poet; Homer never gives himself away like
this. It is true that lines 21–24 above can be construed to mean, "just as
once they taught Hesiod, so now they speak to me," though the weak
conjunction barely bears this construction. Ironically, this question of
identity matters less for the *Theogony,* into which Hesiod hardly again in-
trudes, than for the *Works and Days,* where he is everywhere but is never
named, though his brother and father are.

Hesiod's poems are, of course, not merely autobiographical, though
he is apparent throughout them in a more obvious and explicit sense
than the Delphic oracle's implications about Homer. Yet into the two
topics announced by their titles, the cosmogonic and the day-to-day
practical (what we might call the *Farmer's Almanac* aspect), personal
concerns often intrude. For example, in the following passage, the author
prefaces some detailed advice about sailing offshore with both a dis-
claimer that any Mediterranean peasant of the period would assent to
and an important bit of personal poetic history, his emergence not
merely as a poet but as a prizewinning poet.

I am no expert on nautical matters or nautical vessels,
For I have never by ship sailed over the breadth of the broad sea,
Ever, except to Euboea from Aulis, where the Achaeans
Waited all winter through great storms, till they had marshaled the people
Out of our own holy Hellas to Troy with its beautiful women.
Thence to the games that commemorate wise Amphidamas I voyaged,
Coming at last unto Chalcis's widely advertised contests,
Games that the sons of that brave man had there established. I swear I
Bore off the poetry prize, a tripod with wrought-iron handles,
Which I devoted, of course, to the Muses of Helicon—there first
They had apprised me of clear-voiced music and poetry also.

(*Works and Days*, 638–48)

Here the three strings to Hesiod's lyre are plucked at the same time but not all at the same volume or to the same effect. First, there is the practical matter of seafaring, which he treats immediately hereafter with uncharacteristic modesty. Hesiod was, as far as we can tell—which is as far as he tells us—more a farmer than a fisherman, though these occupations may not have been as distinct then as later and elsewhere. A part-time farmer and a part-time poet, one can assume that he actually followed the plow, not that this made him necessarily a better poet. Then he introduces some mythical material, though he may well have regarded this as historical—as he may have regarded all the phantasmagoria of the *Theogony*. This is the embarkation of the Greek forces for Troy, part of the matter of Homer, which was, of course, common knowledge or belief for centuries to come. And last, but certainly not of least import to the poet, comes the little anecdote about his first prize, an iron pot.

Verse was for millennia the only medium not only of what we consider poetry, so often now divorced from it, but of instruction, for its mnemonic and hopefully memorable qualities. Dactylic hexameter, the meter of Homer and Hesiod, was the most common measure, virtually (given its many uses) a forerunner of prose, which would not be devised, as a literary medium, for centuries. As such it was used for everything from philosophy to medicine and, as in the *Works and Days,* agricultural advice. That composition was oral is thought to be indicated by the formulaic lines and phrases, or set pieces, less common perhaps in Hesiod than Homer, such as the description of the Cyclopses in the *Theogony,* 138–40, where, however, an elegant variation is to be noted.

Save that a singular eye was set in the midst of their foreheads.
Cyclopses were their eponymous nicknames, which is to say, "Round Eyes,"
Seeing a singular circular eye was set in their foreheads.

These poems, particularly, I believe, the *Homeric Hymns,* were not so much written as written down, after an incalculable period of oral transmission, with all the inevitable alterations, including some improvements, attendant upon that. At the same time, it may be wondered how, except metrically, the long lists of names such as that of the Oceanids and Nereids that take up too much of the *Theogony* could be remembered, when writing had been invented for the sake of keeping lists.

It is an insoluble question, like all such with many subjective answers, as to how far in all religious traditions, including one's own, the figures and stories are to be considered literal or allegorical. These, and indeed the whole system to which they belong, are more likely to appear figurative from outside a given worldview. In what light did Hesiod, for instance, think of Prometheus and Pandora, perhaps the only two of his personages to have survived, with their myths, in modern lore? Pandora and her box or jar of mortal ills live as metaphor; Prometheus, the fire bringer, endures in Sophocles, Shelley, and Rockefeller Center. The connection of the two is less well known now, though essential to Hesiod's thinking, whether theological, mythological, or merely poetic.

Clever, sharp-witted Prometheus, and Epimetheus, foolish
From the beginning, pernicious, an evil to bread-eating mortals.

He was the first to receive from Zeus the maiden Pandora,
Whom he had fashioned.

(*Theogony*, 483–86)

Prometheus means "forethought," and his less well-known brother's name means "afterthought"; Pandora, either "she who has been given everything" or "she who gives all," or probably both. The *Works and Days* has more to tell us of Prometheus and Pandora in lines 47–102, a story almost too familiar to need to be summarized: how Zeus punished Prometheus for bringing fire to humans by creating a sort of female golem, who unleashed untold misery on humankind.

Using her fingers, the maid pried open the lid of the great jar,
Sprinkling its contents; her purpose, to bring sad hardships to mankind.
Nothing but Hope stayed there in her stout, irrefrangible dwelling,
Under the lip of the jar, inside, and she never would venture
Outdoors, having the lid of the vessel itself to prevent her,
Willed there by Zeus, who arranges the storm clouds and carries the aegis.
Otherwise, myriad miseries flit round miserable mortals;
Furthermore, full is the earth of much mischief, the deep sea also.
Illnesses visiting humans daily and nightly at all hours
All by themselves bring terrible troubles aplenty to mortals
Silently, seeing their power of speech was suppressed by all-wise Zeus.
There is no way of escaping from Zeus's implacable mind-set.

(*Works and Days*, 91–102)

In support of the notion that the confection of Pandora, if not Prometheus's theft of fire, was as much an invention of Hesiod as of Zeus, one may adduce more than the fact that neither story is related elsewhere. Further evidence lies in the nature of their names, which are too transpicuous and significant. The names of most Greek divinities have no obvious meaning, whatever fanciful etymology may be alleged; they are too old, opaque, and numinous. It is their later epithets—"earth shaking," "laughter loving," "thundering"—that bear the attribute, which is only an attribute and not the essence. The Olympian divinities, such as Zeus, Hera, Apollo, and even Hades, are not mere personifications, though they might later be mistaken for such. It is their forebears whose nomenclature is all too plain: Heaven, Earth, and Mnemosyne or Memory, the mother of the Muses ("Memory bore nine daughters whose hearts were intent upon music" [*Theogony* 58]). But this name sounds like a transparent though perceptive piece of psychologizing—though perhaps not on Hesiod's part—like Themis (Justice) or Eris (Discord). Similarly, the names "Forethought," "Afterthought," and "All-Giving" (or "All-Given") are a giveaway indicating allegorical intent, like "Squire All-worthy," "Benjamin Backbite," or "Doll Tearsheet"; they are too meaningful to have any great traditional, let alone cultic, background. Why then should not our author himself have devised them for his purpose, even though they do not seem to suit that purpose very aptly?

A poet like Hesiod—not that we know any exactly like him—is not merely a passive recipient of lore; he is also an originator, a deviser of metaphorical devices, not always successful. Though the story of the hawk and the nightingale (*Works and Days,* 201–10) has the form of a traditional animal fable—surely one of the oldest of literary forms—it lacks not only a neat applicability to the argument but also the moral in keeping with it that is customary, if not indispensable, to such fables. What performs the function of a moral in the short fable, "Witless is one who attempts to strive against those who are stronger" (208), is not merely defeatist but contradictory to what Hesiod seems to be telling his brother, namely, that Perses should eschew the hubris of the hawk. But if Hesiod is represented by the nightingale as a singer, perhaps the metaphor is less meaningless than it appears at first—and more original. Similarly, the Pandora story and the quasi-traditional scheme of the ages of man (*Works and Days,* 103–77), less hoary on examination than at first appears, are not so contradictory as they seem. Both illustrate, even attempt to explain, in different terms the inevitability of work—*labor omnia vincit*—and human misery generally:

> Formerly dwelt on earth all the various tribes of the human
> Race, on their own and remote from evils and difficult labor
> And from distressing diseases that bring doom closer to each one.

(87–89)

> Truly of iron is this generation, and never by day will
> They intermit hard labor and woe; in the night they will also
> Suffer distress, for the gods will give them unbearable troubles.

(174–76)

Old as it is, this account of human history seems to me to partake more of fiction than myth and to read like the deliberate invention of one poet, like so much in Homer. Did Hesiod see it or, more important, did his audience understand it as more or less allegorical than his account of the birth of the Discords, as personifications rather than allegories or metaphors?

> There is not only one Discord, for on earth she is twofold:
> One of them nobody would find fault with on closer acquaintance;
> One you would deprecate, for they have totally different natures.
> Wickedly, one promotes all the evils of warfare and slaughter;
> No one of humankind likes her; out of necessity, at the
> Will of the blessed immortals, they treat grim Discord with honor.
> There is, moreover, another, the firstborn daughter of dark Night.
> Her did the high-throned scion of Cronus whose home is in heaven
> Place at the roots of the earth; she is certainly better for mankind.
> This is that Discord that stirs up even the helpless to hard work,
> Seeing a man gets eager to work on beholding a neighbor

Who is exceedingly wealthy and makes haste plowing and sowing,
Putting his household in order; so neighbor competing with neighbor
Runs after riches, and therefore this Discord benefits mankind.
Every potter begrudges another, and artists do likewise;
Every beggerman envies a beggar, and poets are rivals.

(*Works and Days*, 11–26)

And how seriously are we meant to take the alternative creation-myth, that of the ages of man, which also had, with variations, long-lived currency? Clearly, as a comparative mythologist Hesiod is no more inconsistent than most creationists, as he traces the moral and material descent of humans in metallic metaphors. A golden age gives way to a silver one, and a bronze age—this with some archaeological resonance—to a heroic period that has no metallic label; at last supervenes the iron age in which we live:

Zeus then created a fifth and last generation of mankind
Such as to this day also inhabit the bountiful green earth.
How I would wish to have never been one of this fifth generation!
Whether I'd died in the past or came to be born in the future.
Truly of iron is this generation, and never by day will
They intermit hard labor and woe; in the night they will also
Suffer distress, for the gods will give them unbearable troubles.
Nevertheless, there will always be good mixed in with the evil.

(*Works and Days*, 170–77)

In the *Works and Days* we are given the name not of the speaker (Hesiod) but of him whom he addresses in various moods, his brother, Perses. Thus this poem belongs to the category of poems directly addressed to a specific or general person or persons, such as the "kings" or magistrates also admonished in it. It is what I would call a second-person or "you" poem, in strong contrast to the third-person poems of Homer, which address or invoke only the gods. This, in fairness, Hesiod also does, albeit briefly: "Come, you Pierian Muses . . ." (*Works and Days,* 1). He also and more mysteriously addresses briefly an undefined second person near the beginning of the *Theogony:* "You, then, let us begin with the Muses." One "you" who surely cannot be meant here is Perses.

Oddly enough, a direct, divine invocation is absent from the poem devoted to the origin of the gods, the *Theogony,* which is as one might expect from its cosmic scope even richer in memorable mythological material than the *Works and Days.* In the latter, the Muses are invoked; in the former, they are merely mentioned. Everyone is familiar with the difference between a performance which involves an audience by addressing it and one which ostensibly ignores it. This difference affects the whole structure and effect of such a performance, and the Hesiodic poems are, at least to begin with, nothing if not performances. The presence of Hesiod's brother, Perses, as the antagonist in the poem is all-important for its effect as well as its purpose, even as its admonitions reach past their putative, named object to all persons in similar circumstances. When the Homeric poems indulge in direct speech, it is within the narrative convention of the poem: character speaks to character, and thus Odysseus tells his extended taradiddle at the court of Alcinoos (*Odyssey,* books 9–12).

The *Theogony* too might be called a third-person poem, envisaging a more general audience—one can hardly say readership at this period, though the text was certainly written down at some early point. It constitutes an archaic encyclopedia or mythological dictionary, arranged not alphabetically—which would imply a readership—but chronologically or, rather, genealogically, genesis or descent being much more calculable than time, except in the day-to-day world treated extensively in the *Works and Days.*

It would seem that the *Theogony* was composed earlier, a piece of virtual juvenilia. Perhaps it was the work Hesiod recited at Chalcis, thereby winning himself not only a cooking pot but a fame which has proved enduring, if not eternal. The *Theogony*'s renown is surely more lasting than he could have conceived and greater than that of the other, lost works with which he is credited, the *Catalogues of Women,* the *Astronomy,* and *Eoiai.*

While the *Homeric Hymns* are impossible to place and date with accuracy, Hesiod's poems anchor him in one place, Boeotia, and one time, the late eighth century BC. Within the aesthetics of the time, originality was not a prime desideratum, though particularity may have been. Classical poetry by definition is imitative, in meter, treatment, and even in subject matter. The greatest Latin poets took their models from Greek: Vergil from Homer, Ovid from (among others) Callimachus, and Horace from melic poets such as Sappho and Alcaeus, avowedly. Even Hesiod had a poetic progeny of sorts, in the *Bucolics,* which Vergil composed before the pseudo-Homeric *Aeneid.* The models of the *Homeric Hymns* are to be found in the longer Homeric poems—hence their name; these were also Hesiod's models in meter and partially in diction—for it seems unlikely that he wrote exactly as he spoke, a purely modern affectation. Poetic diction may be described, and decried, as literally a thing of the past, while eventually much contemporary language will inevitably seem as dated and arch. Hesiod's subject matter must have been just as traditional, though we have no examples of the admonitory genre in Greek before his time. Paradoxically, and fortunately but not fortuitously, genial and not servile imitation results in works of the greatest distinction, whereas too blind an ambition of originality assures only banality and vulgarity in art.

The *Works and Days* is unusual indeed, if not unique among ancient poems in the epic manner and meter, in that, while it encapsulates narrative elements, it does not employ a narrative structure. As such it deprives itself of the compositional devices of story, that most basic form of human discourse, which does not simply put one thing after another in chronological order, but usually involves an element of surprise. That the order of events is not always as straightforward as it appears or as the listener or reader is intended to take it is another and more complex matter. But what then, if it is not narrative, is the nature of the *Works and Days?* Didactic and admonitory, its form is dictated and enforced by its vocative, second-person character: its prime unity depends upon its being directed to a certain person. Within that conversational frame, the organization of topics is extremely loose, free-associational if not haphazard. It is much harder to organize an argument than a tale, as may be seen by the later demand for handbooks of rhetoric, whereas there are none of storytelling, or would not be till our plastic age. Furthermore, as we would all, or most of us, rather listen to a story than to advice, the tales embedded in the *Works and Days* have long outlived the admonishments they were meant to illustrate; one must say "meant," as the connections, like the connections between topics throughout the poem, are most often tenuous. Nevertheless, and for that very reason, I shall attempt a schematic overview to guide the reader through the maze.

Briefly, the poem proceeds from hortatory injunctions to the poet's brother and some "kings" or magistrates to practical advice, principally on farming, addressed to a wider audience. Interspersed within the advice and admonitions are various fables and metaphors, like that of the eagle and the nightingale, which are meant, presumably, to illustrate Hesiod's points but whose applicability is often far from self-evident. The digressions and weak connections throughout the poem give it an inescapable and hardly culpable air of improvisation.

The moral and ethical stance of the poem, however, remains clear. The moral injunctions are simple and familiar, if not incontrovertible. Right, or acting justly, we are told, brings prosperity. Thus, from the very outset, Hesiod's definition of right and justice seems inseparable from self-interest. One other theme is clear in the *Works and Days,* as enunciated in the title, a work ethic that long predates the Protestant.

The other element in the title, the days (of the month—the week was unknown to the Greeks as to the Romans), is dealt with later in the poem, in conjunction with Hesiod's practical advice. Toward the end of the *Works and Days,* Hesiod reverts to a chronological order—one of the oldest besides the tale of personal, human life—that of the husband-man's calendar, the schedule of planting, reaping, and other tasks tied to the seasons. Hesiod and his contemporaries, like people for eons before and centuries after, told time by the sun, the moon, and the stars. Thus, it is natural that a discussion of the archaic calendars—lunar, solar, and sidereal—is attached to his practical advice. Everyday tasks are associated with the empirical astronomy that indicates the seasons, the stellar signs as decisively as the solstices.

"Archaic" rather than merely "ancient" is a term most often used of Hesiod, whose poems were known to the poets of the succeeding, seventh century BC, like those of Homer, though the game of comparative dating is as vexed as it is pointless. Nonetheless, the modern reader, for all Hesiod's old-fashioned, primitive, even fuddy-duddy air, should beware of patronizing this earliest known European poet on the grounds either of historical posteriority or technological superiority. In one form or another his way of doing things would persist for millennia. Furthermore, it requires more skill to make and ply a plow or boat than to drive a combine or motorboat, let alone operate a computer; moreover, the makers of harvesters, speedboats, and computers seldom if ever write poetry. Used as we are to the ideal of progress, which is primarily technological, we shall be surprised if not shocked by Hesiod's regressive, ultraconservative worldview, as expressed most extensively in his account of the ages of man (*Works and Days,* 103–77), where the whole of history hitherto is seen as a decline from a legendary golden age.

First, the immortals who dwell high up on the top of Olympus
Fashioned the firstborn race of articulate men, which was golden,
And it is said that they lived when Cronus was ruling in heaven.
Godlike, they lived like gods, and their hearts were entirely carefree,
Distant strangers to labor and suffering; neither did wretched
Age overtake them; instead, their members intact and unchanged, they
Took much pleasure in banquets and parties, apart from all evils

Till they died as if sleep overcame them. And everything worthwhile
Came to their hand, as the grain-growing earth bore fruit without tilling,
Plenty of good food crops unbegrudged; so they lived at their pleasure,
Peacefully minding their own business, amid numerous good things.
Wealthy in flocks were they and beloved of the blessed immortals.
After this whole first gold generation was finally buried,
Even today they are called pure spirits inhabiting earth and
Noble protectors of mankind, warding off evils from mortals,
Givers of wealth, which royal prerogative still is their business.

(*Works and Days*, 106–21)

This golden age gives way eventually to the grim iron age of the present
and a grimmer future:

... when fathers will differ from children and children from fathers,
Guests with their hosts will differ and comrades will differ with comrades.
And no more will a brother, as previously, be beloved.
When they grow old, people will show no respect to their elders;
Harshly upbraiding them, they use words that are horribly cruel,
Wretches who don't acknowledge the face of the gods and who will not
Pay back ever the cost of their upbringing to their old parents,
Thinking that might means right; and they devastate each other's cities.
There will be nothing like gratitude for oath-keepers and just men,
Nor for the good man; rather, they'll only respect evildoers,
Monsters of violence. Might will be right, all shame will be lost and
All inhibition. The wicked will try to ruin the good man,
Shamelessly uttering falsehoods, wickedly bearing false witness.
Noisy, discordant Envy, malicious, delighting in mischief,
Hateful-faced will accompany all us unfortunate humans.
Self-respect and upright Indignation will go on their way to Olympus,
Quitting the broadly trod earth and concealing their beautiful forms in
Mantles of white, preferring the company of the immortals,

Wholly abandoning mankind, leaving them sorrow and grievous
Pain for the human condition, till there's no ward against evil.

(*Works and Days*, 180–99)

If Hesiod's view of history seems pessimistic, it is arguably more realistic than the foolish, all but universal modernist illusion of superiority to the past. Human beings are, as Hesiod knew so well, inconsistent. The living cannot but feel secretly superior to the dead, much though they might mourn them in private and even revere them in public. Hedging his bets, Hesiod places the heroic age of the Theban and Trojan conflicts between the bronze and iron ages, strongly implying that there is no such heroism now, illustrating the difference between legend and myth.

In the *Theogony*, even more obviously and extensively than in the *Works and Days*, Hesiod is drawing upon and purveying tradition, which is to say, oral mythic material. Here and nowhere else, certainly not in the perfervid imaginations of more modern mythographers, are the sources and limits of that fabulous storehouse on which until quite recently poets have drawn, from Sophocles to Tennyson. For Hesiod such material was, though archaic, not arcane but a living hand-me-down, gossip about the gods. At the same time, though with subsequent interpolations it is hard to tell how much, he muddled and repeated some of his material. The creation of Pandora, whether invented or not, appears here in different words than in the *Works and Days*. For whatever bardic or scribal reasons, the lines about the roots of the world are repeated with great poetic effect:

There in a row all in order the ultimate sources and limits
Stand, of the darkling earth and of nebulous Tartarus, also
Of the unharvested sea as well as the star-studded heavens,
Loathsome, malodorous, foul—and indeed the immortals detest them.

(701–4, 765–68)

There resounds through the poems of Hesiod a sincere commitment, bordering on the naive, unlike the ironic detachment one detects in Homer. The Boeotian really wants to instruct as well as to entertain. It is this didacticism, which differs in kind as well as object from poem to poem, that gives his work its character and its cachet. While the *Homeric Hymns* are in their narrative fashion informative on their divine subjects, they never sound the pedagogic, know-all note. The rhapsodes who recited and in part composed the *Homeric Hymns* were professionals— see book 8 of the *Odyssey;* Hesiod was the consummate amateur, much of his material drawn from his day job as a farmer, and his amateurism shows in the ramshackle construction of his poems.

While one reads Hesiod, if one must, for instruction, one reads the hymns with pleasure, as their original audiences must have listened to them with delight. That those audiences were, we infer, very different from Hesiod's was largely an obvious question of class. Hesiod's hearers would probably have been other agriculturalists, working-class worthies, while the *Homeric Hymns,* like the greater Homeric poems, seem intended for an idler, courtly audience of aristocrats. While we know even less of the authors of the hymns, except that the hymns were authored and did not merely come into oral being, we may suppose them to have been professional bards, perhaps peripatetic, whereas Hesiod had a farm to run.

Another difference between Hesiod and "Homer" is the treatment, even the selection of the gods who loom so large in both their poems. It is only toward the end of the *Theogony* (900ff) that Hesiod deals with the Olympian pantheon who form the subject matter of the hymns as of so much later poetry. There is, moreover, a discernible alteration of tone toward the divine beings, the Homeric one being more familiar and playful, while still worshipful.

Even more playful, indeed parodic, is the tone of *The Battle of the Frogs and the Mice,* whose burlesque character bespeaks its date as late or at least later, however vaguely so, since a parody always postdates its model, in this case the *Iliad*. Some parts may even be Byzantine, but there are few ancient Greek poems of which this may not be alleged.

In translating these poems, I have attempted, so far as our very different languages allow, an equivalent meter in English: equivalent meters, I should say, that of the Hesiodic poems more rough and irregular, with more "substitutions" than the smooth, flowing measures of the Homeric poems. Homeric in light of their approximate period and style, these would hardly be called hymns nowadays but lays, prologues, even epyllia. The formulary element, more conspicuous in Homer than Hesiod, I have handled variously and without undue, superstitious regard.

> Phoebus, the swan sings of you with clear note and with musical wing-beats
> . . . you does the rhapsode whose diction is pleasant remember
> Always to sing first and last as he handles his resonant lyre.

HESIOD

WORKS AND DAYS

THEOGONY

WORKS AND DAYS

Come, you Pierian[1] Muses, who give us the glory of music,   1
Tell me of Zeus, your progenitor, make praise-songs in his honor;
Through him, moreover, are humankind undistinguished or famous,
They are sung or unsung by the will of omnipotent great Zeus.
Easily making a man strong, easily he overthrows him,   5
Easily humbles the proud as he lifts up high the obscure, and
Easily straightens the crooked as well as deflating the puffed-up—
Zeus, who is deathless and thunders aloft and dwells in the highest.
Listen to me and behold, make straight your decisions with justice.
I would be happy to speak true facts to you, Perses,[2] my brother.   10

There is not only one Discord, for on earth she is twofold:
One of them nobody would find fault with on closer acquaintance;
One you would deprecate, for they have totally different natures.
Wickedly, one promotes all the evils of warfare and slaughter;
No one of humankind likes her; out of necessity, at the   15
Will of the blessed immortals, they treat grim Discord with honor.
There is, moreover, another, the firstborn daughter of dark Night.
Her did the high-throned scion of Cronus whose home is in heaven
Place at the roots of the earth; she is certainly better for mankind.
This is that Discord that stirs up even the helpless to hard work,   20

---

1. From Pieria in Macedonia, one of the many homes of the Muses, like Mount Helicon and Mount Parnassus, nearer Hesiod's home.
2. Otherwise unknown. Note on pronunciation: a last or next to last *e* is sounded, as in *Perses* and as in many feminine names, such as *Phoebe* and *Hermione*.

Seeing a man gets eager to work on beholding a neighbor
Who is exceedingly wealthy and makes haste plowing and sowing,
Putting his household in order; so neighbor competing with neighbor
Runs after riches, and therefore this Discord benefits mankind.

25 Every potter begrudges another, and artists do likewise;
Every beggarman envies a beggar, and poets are rivals.

Perses, be sure you deposit these things in your heart and your spirit,
Lest Discord, which is given to mischief, distract you from work and
You begin sneaking about, eavesdropping on feuds in the forum.

30 You have no business getting in fights and disputing in public,
Not if you haven't sufficient for life laid up in your storeroom,
Seasonal fruits of the earth, ripe grain of abundant Demeter.
When you have plenty of that, turn freely to fierce competition
For the possessions of others; no second chance will be yours to

35 Do so. Let us however decide our disputes by means of impartial
Judgments, for justice derives from Zeus and is bound to be perfect.
When we had split our inheritance, you grabbed most of it, making
Off with it, to enhance the repute of our bribe-hungry royal
Masters, who love to adjudge such cases as ours in their courtrooms.

40 Idiots! They don't know how much more is the half than the whole, nor
What is the use of a diet of mallow and asphodel,[3] Perses?

Plainly the gods keep secret from humankind the means of survival;
Otherwise, you in a day could easily do enough work to
Last you a whole year long, and without any further exertion.

45 Soon, very soon you would hang up over the fireplace your rudder;
Then would be finished the labors of oxen and hard-working donkeys.
No, Zeus kept it a secret because in his heart he was angry,
Seeing how devious-minded Prometheus once had fooled him;
Therefore did almighty Zeus plot sorrows and troubles for mankind.

3. Weeds, greens.

He hid fire, which, however, then Iapetus's great-hearted son, to   50
Benefit humankind, pilfered from Zeus, the purveyor of counsel,
Hid in a hollowed-out stalk to baffle the lover of thunder.

Then cloud-gathering Zeus to Prometheus said in his anger:
"Iapetus's brat, since you're so much smarter than anyone else, you're
Happy to outwit me, and rejoice in the fire you have stolen—   55
For yourself a calamity, also for men of the future.
For I shall give them a bad thing, too, in exchange for this fire, which
Heartily all may delight in, embracing a homegrown evil."
Speaking, the father of gods and of mankind exploded in laughter.
Then he commanded Hephaestus,[4] the world-famed craftsman, as   60
     soon as
Possible to mix water and earth, and infuse in it human
Speech, also strength, and to make it look like a goddess, and give it
Likewise a girl-like form that was pretty and lovesome. Athena
Would instruct her in handwork and weaving of intricate fabrics;
Furthermore, gold Aphrodite[5] should drip charm over her head to   65
Cause heartsore longing, emotional anguish exhausting the body.
Zeus gave instructions to Hermes, the sure guide, slayer of Argus,[6]
To put in her the heart of a bitch and a devious nature.
Then did the famed lame god manufacture at once from the earth a
Fair simulacrum of one shy maiden, according to Zeus's will.   70
Next to her skin did the godlike Graces and gracious Persuasion
Carefully place gold necklaces; round her adorable head the
Hours who are gorgeously coiffed wove garlands of beautiful spring
     flowers.
Hermes, our sure guide, slayer of Argus, contrived in her breast
Lies and misleadingly false words joined to a devious nature,   75

4. Vulcan in Latin, the god of workmanship.
5. Venus in Latin, the goddess of love.
6. A many-eyed monster, which Hermes killed. It became a peacock. We still say
"argus-eyed."

At the behest of the deep-voiced thunderer, Zeus; and the herald
God of the gods then gave her a voice. And he called her Pandora,
Seeing how all who inhabit lofty Olympus had given
Something to pretty Pandora, that giant bane to industrious mankind.

80 When he had finished this downright desperate piece of deception,
To Epimetheus Zeus then dispatched the slayer of Argus,
Famed swift messenger of the immortals, with her as a present.
But Epimetheus had forgotten Prometheus's warning,
Not to accept anything from Olympian Zeus, but to send it
85 Back where it came from, lest it become a disaster for mortals.
Once he'd accepted it, he, possessing the bane, recognized it.

Formerly dwelt on earth all the various tribes of the human
Race, on their own and remote from evils and difficult labor
And from distressing diseases that bring doom closer to each one.
90 For in misfortune do humans age rapidly, quicker than ever.
Using her fingers, the maid pried open the lid of the great jar,
Sprinkling its contents; her purpose, to bring sad hardships to
    mankind.
Nothing but Hope stayed there in her stout, irrefrangible dwelling,
Under the lip of the jar, inside, and she never would venture
95 Outdoors, having the lid of the vessel itself to prevent her,
Willed there by Zeus, who arranges the storm clouds and carries the
    aegis.[7]
Otherwise, myriad miseries flit round miserable mortals;
Furthermore, full is the earth of much mischief, the deep sea also.
Illnesses visiting humans daily and nightly at all hours
100 All by themselves bring terrible troubles aplenty to mortals
Silently, seeing their power of speech was suppressed by all-wise Zeus.
There is no way of escaping from Zeus's implacable mind-set.

7. Stock epithet whose meaning is obscure: "who carries the goatskin"? "Who fol-
lows the lapwing or snipe that presages a storm"? We say "under the aegis of."

If you prefer, an alternate story[8] I'll summarize also
Well and expertly, and lay it up in your mind and preserve it—
Namely, the common origin shared by immortals and mortals.   105
First, the immortals who dwell high up on the top of Olympus
Fashioned the firstborn race of articulate men, which was golden,
And it is said that they lived when Cronus was ruling in heaven.
Godlike, they lived like gods, and their hearts were entirely carefree,
Distant strangers to labor and suffering; neither did wretched   110
Age overtake them; instead, their members intact and unchanged, they
Took much pleasure in banquets and parties, apart from all evils
Till they died as if sleep overcame them. And everything worthwhile
Came to their hand, as the grain-growing earth bore fruit without
    tilling,
Plenty of good food crops unbegrudged; so they lived at their pleasure,   115
Peacefully minding their own business, amid numerous good things.
Wealthy in flocks were they and beloved of the blessed immortals.
After this whole first gold generation was finally buried,
Even today they are called pure spirits inhabiting earth and
Noble protectors of mankind, warding off evils from mortals,   120
Givers of wealth, which royal prerogative still is their business.

Afterward, those that inhabit Olympus fashioned a second,
Silver race, which was very inferior, worse than the first one,
For they did neither in growth nor intellect equal the golden.
Children were then brought up by their diligent mothers a hundred   125
Years and engaged in sheer infantile child's play there in their own
    homes.
But when maturing at last they came to the measure of manhood
They lived only the tiniest time, and moreover they suffered

8. There is no earlier source for this account of human history in Greek, as there is
nothing earlier than Hesiod, but parallel versions exist in Persian, Sanskrit, Babylonian,
and Hebrew (for instance, Daniel 2:31ff).

Much in their folly; they could not keep themselves back from their
    wicked
130 Violence on one another; nor were they willing to serve the immortals
Or make sacrifice using the Blessed Ones' sacrosanct altars,
As it is lawful for humans to do and according to custom.
Thereupon, Zeus, son of Cronus, suppressed them all in his anger,
Seeing they did not worship the gods who inhabit Olympus.
135 And when this generation of silver in turn was interred
Under the earth, they were termed blessed spirits although they were
    mortal,
Second in time, yet everywhere honor is also their portion.

Zeus manufactured a new third race of articulate mankind,
But this bronze generation in no way equaled the silver,
140 For they were offspring of ash trees, mighty and frightful, and Ares'
Noisy employment concerned them and violent deeds. They ate no
Bread and appeared tough-minded as adamant, wholly unpolished;
All too great was their strength and their hands were invincible,
    growing
Out of their mighty shoulders to hang at the end of their stout limbs.
145 Bronze was their armor and brazen their arms, brass-bound were their
    dwellings;
Bronze were the tools which they worked with, as iron had not been
    invented.
Dying by each other's hands, they went down to the underworld's cold
    rot,
Leaving no names to posterity. Black death took them despite their
Physical strength, and they quit altogether the luminous sunlight.
150 But when this bronze generation, however, was finally buried,
Zeus, son of Cronus, created a whole new fourth generation
Here on the fertile earth who were better and fonder of justice;
This was a godlike race of heroical men who were known as
Demigods, last generation before our own on the broad earth.

Horrible war with its frightening war cries wholly destroyed them,   155
Some who fought in the kingdom of Cadmus below seven-gated
Thebes where they strove in vain with each other for Oedipus's rich
    flocks,[9]
Others transported across the immense deep gulf of the sea on
Shipboard to Troy after well-coiffed Helen, the fairest of women.[10]
Some of them there death's ending completely enveloped in darkness.   160
Others, however, the son of Cronus decided to grant a
Dwelling place far from men at the furthermost ends of the earth, and
There they continue to live, their consciousness perfectly carefree,
There in the Isles of the Blessed, beside deep-eddying Ocean,[11]
Distant from the immortals; and Cronus was king of that kingdom   165
After the father of gods and of men freed him from his bondage;
Now from those heroes he gets high honor as is most befitting.
Fortunate heroes! Their plowlands are so fertile they yield a
Crop more delicious than honey that flourishes three times yearly.
Zeus then created a fifth and last generation of mankind   170
Such as to this day also inhabit the bountiful green earth.
How I would wish to have never been one of this fifth generation!
Whether I'd died in the past or came to be born in the future.
Truly of iron is this generation, and never by day will
They intermit hard labor and woe; in the night they will also   175
Suffer distress, for the gods will give them unbearable troubles.
Nevertheless, there will always be good mixed in with the evil.
Zeus will destroy this race of articulate mankind, however,

---

9. The sons of King Oedipus fought over their patrimony in front of Thebes, which was founded by Cadmus.

10. When Helen was abducted by the Trojan prince Paris, her husband Menelaus marshaled the armies of Greece to reclaim her, thus launching the Trojan war. This and the preceding reference are to stories current before Hesiod's day, part of his poetic patrimony, also the material of poetry long afterward.

11. An alternative abode of the dead, usually reserved for heroes, distinct from the underworld, the house of Hades, or Tartarus. In Hesiod's time the known world was surrounded by the stream of Ocean, the father of waters.

When they have come to exhibit at birth gray hairs at their temples
180 And when fathers will differ from children and children from fathers,
Guests with their hosts will differ and comrades will differ with
comrades.
And no more will a brother, as previously, be beloved.
When they grow old, people will show no respect to their elders;
Harshly upbraiding them, they use words that are horribly cruel,
185 Wretches who don't acknowledge the face of the gods and who will not
Pay back ever the cost of their upbringing to their old parents,
Thinking that might means right; and they devastate each other's cities.
There will be nothing like gratitude for oath-keepers and just men,
Nor for the good man; rather, they'll only respect evildoers,
190 Monsters of violence. Might will be right, all shame will be lost and
All inhibition. The wicked will try to ruin the good man,
Shamelessly uttering falsehoods, wickedly bearing false witness.
Noisy, discordant Envy, malicious, delighting in mischief,
Hateful-faced will accompany all us unfortunate humans.
195 Self-respect and upright Indignation will go on their way to Olympus,
Quitting the broadly trod earth and concealing their beautiful forms in
Mantles of white, preferring the company of the immortals,
Wholly abandoning mankind, leaving them sorrow and grievous
Pain for the human condition, till there's no ward against evil.
200 Now I shall tell you a fable for kings who have understanding.
A hawk spoke to a speckle-necked nightingale cruelly, as he
Lifted her up to the clouds while gripping her tight in his talons.
Piteously she, transfixed by his crooked claws, was lamenting
When the imperious hawk addressed her in arrogant parlance,
205 "Why, little lady, such shrieks? One stronger than you now has got you;
Where you are going, I'll take you myself, though you are a songstress,
For as I please I'll make you my dinner or give you your freedom.
Witless is one who attempts to strive against those who are stronger.
When he is stripped of the prize it is injury added to insult."
210 Thus said the fast-flying hawk, that bird with the generous wingspan.

Pay more attention to Justice and curb high-handedness, Perses;
Violence ill suits men who are lowly; not even the noble
Man can lightly endure it; it weighs on a person who's fallen
Into affliction. It's better to take your way on the other
Road which conduces to right. For outrage surrenders to justice   215
When they arrive at discrete ends. Fools understand this the hard way.
Oath every step of the way keeps up with dishonest misjudgments.
There is a tumult when Justice is dragged where men who are venal
Hijack her, those who impose false judgments with crooked injustice.
Weeping, she visits a city and seeks out haunts of the people,   220
Dimly enveloped in mist, she's bringing misfortune to humans.
Those who have driven her out do not behave to her rightly.
Others deliver correct just judgments to stranger and fellow
Countryman, never transgressing a bit the way of the righteous;
Theirs is a stalwart city and flourishing people within it.   225
Peace that cherishes children is over the land, and all-seeing
Zeus never ever allots them cruel and terrible warfare.
Neither disasters nor famines befall men just in their dealings;
At their convivial banquets they eat the fruits of their labors.
Earth bears plentiful food for them; plenty of oaks on the mountains   230
Bear on their summit plentiful acorns, and bees in their center.
Beautifully woolly their sheep are, fraught with luxuriant fleece. Their
Women at term give birth to fine children resembling their fathers.
Always they flourish with all good things, but they never on shipboard
Venture; the grain-growing plowland provides them produce in plenty.   235

Zeus, son of Cronus, who sees far and wide, metes justice to those who
Care for evil and violence, foster criminal actions;
Time and again whole cities are lost on account of one wicked
Man who is sinful and dreams up deeds of presumptuous daring.
Zeus, son of Cronus, from heaven inflicts great suffering on them,   240
Famine and pestilence at once, making the populace perish;
Women do not give birth, so that households diminish in number,

All through the plans of Olympian Zeus, who likewise at other
Times devastates broad armies of men and their fortifications,
245 And in his wrath Cronus's son sinks ships in the midst of the sea, too.

Princes, behold for yourselves how just is this heavenly justice,
For the immortals are closer than you suppose to the actions of
    humans,
Closely observing how some of us, steeped in crooked injustice,
Grind one another right down, not minding the gods' indignation,
250 For on the bountiful earth there are thrice ten thousand immortal
Spies in the service of Zeus to watch over men who are mortal.
They watch just judgments and villainous deeds at the same time.
Dimly enveloped in mist, they wander all over the broad earth.
Maidenly Justice moreover exists, Zeus's virginal daughter,
255 Honored, respected among those gods who inhabit Olympus.
Should anyone by dishonest speech disrespect and offend her,
She will immediately sit down next to her father, the son of
Cronus, and tattle to him of unjust men's hearts, till the people
Pay for the mindless follies of rulers who, consciously wicked,
260 Like to subvert just judgments with sentences woefully crooked.
Rulers, be careful of matters like this; make straight your
    pronouncements,
Greedy for gifts though you are, and rescind your dishonest decisions.
He's only harming himself who's bent upon harming another;
Evil designs do the most harm always to workers of evil.
265 Zeus's all-seeing omniscient eye can see even these if it wishes,
Noticing also what sort of justice a city contains. But
Anyway may neither I nor my son be "just" among men if
Rascals pretend to be "just"; men more in the wrong get
Better decisions. But all-wise Zeus would, I hope, not permit it.
270 Brother Perses, lay up in your heart these things that I tell you:
Paying attention to righteousness, forget about force altogether.
Zeus, son of Cronus, ordained one rule of behavior for humans

But quite another for fishes and animals, likewise for birds, who
Commonly eat one another; there's no fair play in such creatures.
Men received justice, by far best quality ever conceived; to   275
That man who argues a just cause truthfully, knowing its justice,
Zeus the far seeing will give great blessings, prosperity, good luck,
But for someone who knowingly bears false witness, committing
Perjury, injuring justice, and doing permanent damage,
Surely his progeny will be left in the shadows hereafter,   280
Whereas the race of the faithful man will be better hereafter.
Perses, you idiot, knowing a thing or two will instruct you.
Wickedness may be obtained too easily and in abundance,
Smooth is the road to her dwelling; indeed she lives very nearby.
But in the way of access to virtue, immortals have placed the   285
Sweat of our brows, and the pathway there is both lengthy and steep and
Rough and uneven at first; when at last one comes to the summit,
Then it is easy enough, though difficult still up to that point.
Best of all is the man who, considering every thing himself,
Now understands what things are thereafter and finally better;   290
Similarly he is wise who listens to expert advisers.
One who's unable to think for himself or listen to others,
Storing their words in his heart, that person is perfectly useless.
You on the other hand, Perses, remember forever my earnest
Precepts, and work, you descendant of Zeus, work hard, so that hunger   295
Loathes you and shuns you, and may rich-garlanded, honored Demeter
Kindly befriend you and fill your granary yearly with foodstuffs.
Hunger is always the boon best friend of a man who is shiftless.
Even the gods are disgusted, like men, with a chap who is lazy,
Living in idleness, like drones lacking a stinger to sting with,   300
Wholly exhausting the labors of bees by being voracious,
Shirking all work. But care for your labors and put them in order,
So may your granaries fill up quickly with seasonal produce.
Men by the work of their hands get plenty of sheep and are wealthy;
Someone who does hard work is a favorite of the immortals,   305

Also of mortals, for both of them hate sincerely the idle.
Labor is far from disgraceful. Indeed, unemployment's disgraceful,
And if you work hard, those who are idle will quickly begin to
Envy your wealth, for honor and worth are attendant on riches.
310 No matter what your condition, to work hard always is better.
If you can tear your misguided mind from another's possessions,
Turn your attention to work; yes, mind your own business, I tell you.
Modesty's no bad companion for one who is needy.
Modesty can at the same time bother and benefit mankind.
315 Modesty goes with misfortune as arrogance goes with good fortune.
Things are not there to be taken, no, wealth god-given is better.
If one gets hold of immense good fortune by physical force or
Steals it away with a lying tongue, as is often the case when
Lust for profit deceives the intelligence given to mankind
320 And when immodesty shamelessly casts out modesty wholly,
Readily heaven obscures that man and diminishes his house;
Only the shortest while does good fortune attend the dishonest.
Equally bad is the man who does wrong to a supplicant or a
Guest, or who guiltily goes upstairs to the bed of his brother,
325 Furtively lying in lust with that brother's wife, which is sinful,
Or who irrationally offends against fatherless children,
Or who disputes with his aged father on age's unhappy
Threshold, assailing the old man mercilessly with severe words.
With such a man even Zeus is irate, at last for the wicked
330 Doings of mortals exacting an ultimate harsh retribution.
See you exclude such deeds from your idiot heart altogether,
And insofar as you can, make sacrifice to the immortals
Blandly, with ritual purity, likewise burning the fat meats.
Gladden the deathless gods with libations and incense at all times,
335 Both upon going to bed and at the return of the holy
Light, so they'll grant you a tranquil heart and a satisfied spirit;
So you can bid on your neighbor's plot and not he on your own land.
Summon your friend to a feast; pass over your enemy rudely;

Summon above all the neighbor living the nearest to your place,
For should something or other occur on your property sometime,   340
Neighbors will come as they are, while in-laws are putting their coats on.
A bad neighbor's a curse just as much as a good one's a blessing;
Anyone gets good value who has a respectable neighbor.
Hardly an ox would get lost but for malevolent neighbors.
Borrow fair measure from neighbors, and pay them back in proportion   345
With an identical measure, and more, just as much as you're able.
Thus, if you're ever in need, you'll have somebody you can depend on.
Do not procure base gain, for a gain that is base is a dead loss.
One who befriends you, befriend, and someone who visits you, visit;
Give to a person who gives, but not to a person who doesn't: 350
Everyone gives to the open-handed but none to the stingy.
Giving's a good wife; grasping's a bad wife, death is her dowry;
Therefore, the man who gives willingly gives magnificently and
Comes to rejoice in his own gift, taking delight in his bounty,
Whereas the man who, prompted by shamelessness, seizes another's   355
Goods, be they ever so small, his heart will be thoroughly frozen.
If you continue to add a little amount to a little,
And if you do so quite often, that little will soon be a whole lot:
He who augments what he has can ward off the furies of hunger.
None of the stuff that a man lays up in his house will distress him;   360
Everything's better at home, outdoors is a dangerous region.
It is a fine thing to take what's available; wanting what's not brings
Anguish of mind and a heartfelt grief, which I bid you consider.
Drink your fill of the cask newly broached and when nearly finished;
Ration the stuff in the middle, the dregs make a horrible mouthful.   365
See that the wages you promise a faithful retainer are paid soon.
And with a brother be sure to smile, and in front of a witness,
Certainly trust and distrust prove equally fatal to mankind.
Don't let a wily, wheedling woman who wiggles her bottom
Wholly befuddle your wits: her purpose is rifling your pantry.   370
One who believes in a woman believes in cheats and deceivers.

Let there be only one heir, his paternal inheritance's steward,
Who will fatten it up so that wealth will augment in the household.
You should be careful to die old if you are leaving a grandson;
375 Easily Zeus will provide inexhaustible wealth to your increase:
Greater attention to labor by many enlarges the profit.
If your desire for wealth is engrained in the depths of your being,
Do as I tell you, and work, work, work, never cease from your labors.

Just as soon as the Pleiades,[12] daughters of Atlas, have risen,
380 Gather your harvest; begin to plow when those sisters are setting.
For forty nights and days is this bright constellation occluded,
Till, when the year has in part completed its annual cycle,
They reappear in the heavens at sunrise: time then to sharpen your
sickle.
This, it appears, is the rule that governs the plains and all those who
385 Live by the seashore, also all those who inhabit the glens and
Hillsides remote from the billowing sea, rich country to live in:
Straight from your bed, without troubling to dress, plow, sow, and nude
harvest,
If you are eager to do the work of Demeter in due time,
So that everything reaches its seasonal growth, lest hereafter,
390 Being in want, you go begging next door and return empty-handed.
So have you recently come to me, too, you idiot Perses.
I will not give any more, no more than your usual portion.
Work, silly Perses, work, for the gods have assigned it to mankind,
Otherwise you and your children and wife will go to your neighbors,
Begging your living, bitter in heart, and they'll pay no attention.
395 Two, three times you'll be lucky, but if you should further harass them
You will not get what you want, though talking much vain and inane
talk.

12. A constellation, the seven sisters, whose name is derived from the Greek verb "to sail," as their rising signaled the sailing season.

All of your eloquence comes to nothing, and so I beseech you,
Think about paying your pressing debts and escaping from hunger.
First of all, purchase a house and a woman, an ox for the plowing,   400
That is, a woman to own, not to marry, who'll follow the oxen.[13]
Tidily keep all the goods in your house shipshape and all ready,
Lest you must ask of another and he say no, so you live in
Want, and the seasons go by and your agriculture is ruined.
Do not postpone your work till tomorrow and after tomorrow;   405
Men who are idle at work don't fill up their barns with abundance,
Nor do men who procrastinate. Industry benefits labor.
Someone who puts off labor will evermore wrestle with ruin.
When the unbearable strength of the sun abates and its sweaty
Heat, and omnipotent Zeus sends mortals the downpours of Autumn,   410
Then the complexions of humans feel comfortable—quite an
    improvement!
Sirius[14] briefly by day floats over the heads of devoted
Men but is visible more in the nighttime. Wood that you cut when
Leaves are bestrewing the ground and growth is arrested is worm-free.
Do not forget woodcutting, this season's for plying the hatchet.   415
Chisel a mortar that's three feet long and a pestle of five feet;
Also an axle that's seven feet long will prove mighty handy,
Or, if you fashion it eight feet long, you can carve out a mallet.
Whittle a wheel two feet and a half for a wagon of two foot
Three. There is plenty of bent firewood. If you come on a tree fork   420
Fit for a plow, bring it home with you, when you have looked on the
    mountains
And in the fields for a holm oak, strongest for plowing with oxen,
After some hand of Athena's[15] has fastened it tight to the plowshare,
Pegging the business end to the handle. So keep in the house two

13. Slavery was, of course, common in Hesiod's day, as it was in many societies until
quite recently.
  14. The dog-star, conspicuous at high summer, in hot weather.
  15. A skilled workman.

425 Plows you are working on, one with a natural bent and the other
    Joined artificially, for that scheme is undoubtedly better:
    If you should break one plow you can yoke up the ox to the other.
    Handles of laurel and elm are most likely totally worm-free,
    So is a plowshare of oak as well as a plow-tree of holm oak.
430 Get two oxen, two bulls about nine years of age, when their strength is
    Still at its peak in the prime of their age: such are excellent workers,
    Nor will they fight one another in plowland, smashing the plow to
    Pieces, and bringing your hard agricultural labor to nothing.
    Let them be followed by some energetic farmworker of forty
435 Years, who has broken his fast with a quarter loaf of eight slices[16]
    And will attend to his work while driving the straightest of furrows,
    Having no time for glancing askance at his comrades; he keeps his
    Mind on his work, for better by far a grown man as a partner,
    Who's better at scattering seeds and doesn't keep scattering double;
440 While immature young men are too often intrigued with each other.

    Every year when you hear the shrill din of the cranes from the clouds,
        take
    Note, for it signals the season to plow, indicating the rainy
    Wintertime, gnawing the heart of the man who possesses no oxen.
    Now's the appropriate time for feeding up long-horned cattle
445 Indoors, for it's easy to ask for a team and a wagon,
    Easier still to refuse: "I've plenty of work for my oxen."
    Thick are the wits of the man who says that his wagon's already
    Finished; the fool doesn't know there are hundreds of planks in a wagon.
    Make it your business to have these planks in your house for the future.

450 Then, when the time for plowing at last is apparent to mortals,
    That is the hour to hurry, yourself and your servants together,
    Whether in wet or in dry, to plow at the season of plowing,

16. They did not, of course, have sliced bread then, but broke it off the whole loaf.

Rouse yourself early, get up, so your field will soon be overflowing.
Turn up the soil in the spring; then summer won't be disappointing.
Sow your seed in the fallow land when it is looser and lighter.   455
Fallow land wards agricultural ruin off, charms little children.
Beg subterranean Zeus, pray to Demeter the holy
That the perfected and sacred grains of Demeter be weighty.
When you're beginning the plowing at first, then hold in your hand the
End of the tail of the plow, lay stripes on the backs of your oxen,   460
Pulling the peg by the straps. While walking a little behind, a
Serf with a mattock creates much trouble and woe for the birds by
Hiding the seed in the ground. Good husbandry, that is the best for
Men who are mortal, as rotten husbandry is the most evil.
So will the heads of your wheat hang down to the ground in their   465
    fullness,
If the Olympian gives you a good outcome; after all, then
Dusting your storage jars you'll be brushing off cobwebs, I hope that
You will rejoice when you've got your livelihood safe in your keeping;
So, well-provided, you'll come to misty spring. And you'll look to
Nobody else, but another may likely need your assistance.   470
Yet if you plow the excellent earth at the winter solstice,
Squatting you'll reap, and you'll harvest by hand but a pitiful handful,
Binding the dust-covered sheaves all askew. You'll not be too happy
Bringing them home in a basket, when not very many admire you.
Truly the purposes vary of Zeus, who carries the aegis,   475
All too difficult are they to fathom by men who are mortal.
If you insist upon plowing too late, one remedy there is:
After the cuckoo is heard for the first time loud in the oak tree's
Foliage, cheering mankind all over the earth, which is boundless,
If on the third day Zeus begins raining and doesn't let up till   480
Rain neither rises above cows' hooves nor is very much under,
Then one who's late with his plowing will rival him who was early.
Keep this advice, every bit of it, well in mind, and forget not
Either the mist-gray days of the spring or the rain-sodden season.

485 Pass by the blacksmith's forge with its cozy and comfortable clubroom
During the winter, when cold prevents a man doing his outdoor
Work, at the time when laborious men do most for their households,
Lest in its terrible helplessness one bad winter surprise you
Stricken with poverty, scratching a swollen foot with a hand that is
skinny.

490 Every man unemployed who waits upon hope, though it's empty,
Lacking a livelihood, grimly meditates plenty of evil.
Hope is no good that accompanies men who are poverty stricken,
Men who relax at the club, whose living is highly uncertain.[17]
While it is still midsummer, be sure to instruct your domestics,

495 "It will not always be summer; it's time to build yourselves shelters."
Skip the whole month of Lenaion,[18] those harsh days ready to take the
Skin off an ox, and the frost which becomes so ruthlessly cruel
Every time that the north wind, Boreas, blows on the good earth.
When over horse-training Thrace[19] aloft, agitating the broad sea,

500 Boreas blows, he awakes both forest and earth in an uproar,
Falling upon many tall, leafy oaks and bristling fir trees
Growing in groves on the mountains; he brings them crashing to earth,
and
All of the endless, immense great forest resounds with the impact.
Animals shudder and tuck their tails in between their hind legs,

505 Even the ones whose hide is covered with fur, for the north wind,
Cold as it is, blows through them although they are terribly hairy,
And it can penetrate even the hide of a bull, which can't stop it.
Also it blows through the goat's fine hairs, but the fleece of a sheep it
Cannot, because it is so close-packed that the powerful north wind

510 Can't penetrate it, which nonetheless easily bowls over old men.
Nor is it able to penetrate smooth-skinned virginal maidens

17. Hesiod and his like, as far as we can tell from the poem and only from the poem, were free, landowning, modest agriculturalists, neither serfs nor gentleman farmers.
18. Midwinter.
19. North and northeast, roughly the Balkans and Romania.

As they abide in the house beside their affectionate mothers,
Blissfully ignorant still of the doings of gold Aphrodite.
They, after carefully washing their delicate bodies in water,
Slickly anointed with oil, lie down in the innermost private   515
Room, on a wintry day when the boneless octopus gnaws his
Foot in his home without fire, in his wretchedly humid apartment.[20]
Nor does the sun indicate fresh pasturage for a beginning,
Wandering, rather, over the countries and cities of black men,
Shining, however more sluggishly, on all Hellenes at the solstice.   520
Then both the horned and the hornless inhabitants of the wild
     woodland
Flee through the thickets and groves with pathetically chattering teeth
     and
All of them have in their hearts and their minds one single desire, while
Searching for shelter, to find some large, hollow rock or some thickset
Covert, and like a three-legged[21] man whose back is so bent it appears 525
Broken, whose face is moreover directed perpetually downward,
Like this old man, beasts wander at random, avoiding the white snow.
Furthermore, take my advice, put on for your body's protection
A soft cloak and a tunic that comes all the way down to your ankles,
Woven of thickest woof on top of the thinnest of warp threads.   530
Wrap yourself up in this garb, your hairs will not quiver with cold and
Bristle and stand up on end all over your shivering body.
Tie on your feet boots made of the hide of an ox freshly slaughtered,
Make them close-fitting and snug with a lining of felt on the inside.
And when the season of cold is at hand, get out a few kid skins,   535
Sew them together with sinews of oxen in order to throw them
Over your back to protect you from rain; on top of your head a
Felt cap cunningly made to prevent you from getting your ears wet.

---

20. A rare example of Hesiod's flight of fancy.
21. That is, supporting himself on a stick; a reference to the riddle of the Sphinx to Oedipus.

Cold is the dawn when the north wind briskly commences its blowing;
540 Daily at sunrise a luminous mist spreads over the earth from
Star-spangled heaven and covers the fields of fortunate mortals,
Moisture drawn up from the rivers that go on flowing forever;
High it is lifted above the earth by tempestuous windstorms.
Sometimes it rains toward evening, sometimes it turns very windy,
545 Driven by Boreas blowing from Thrace, who disperses the thick clouds.
Finish your labors beforehand, hastily make your way homeward,
Lest an umbrageous cloud from the sky should envelope you sometime,
Soaking your body with ice cold moisture and drenching your clothing.
This you should surely avoid; this month is the hardest and harshest,
550 Wintry and cruel to livestock, cruel to men in addition.
This is the season to give your cattle a half of their rations,
More to your workman: long are the nights, although kindly and useful.
Take good care of such things till the annual round is concluded
And days finally equal the nights in duration, when again will
555 Earth, who is mother of all, produce all her various first fruits.
Soon after Zeus has completed the wintry sixty days since the
Solstice, Arcturus,[22] forsaking the sacred river of Ocean,
First climbs brilliantly shining above the penumbra of evening.
Following after this star, King Pandion's daughter, the swallow[23]
560 Twittering shrilly emerges for men when the spring is beginning.
Pruning your vineyard is better before the swallow's appearance.
But when the snail with its portable domicile climbs up the plants from
Earth as it hides from the Pleiades—too late to dig up your vineyard,
Rather it's time to sharpen your sickle and rouse your serfs in the
    morning.
565 Shun comfy seats in the shade, shun lying abed until sunrise
During the season of harvest when sunlight burns your complexion:

22. A star, "the bear-warden," which rises in early spring.
23. In another old story, Pandion's daughter Philomela was turned into a swallow.
See Ovid, *Metamorphoses*, book 6.

Then you should busy yourself to bring home agricultural produce,
Getting up early to make quite sure that your livelihood's certain.
For early morning accounts for a good third part of your work day.
Morning advances a man on his way and advances his labor;   570
Morning's appearance advances so many men on their journey;
Morning's the hour for putting the yokes upon all of your oxen.

After the artichoke flowers and one-note grasshoppers sitting
Up in the leaves pour forth their melodious high-pitched singsong
Constantly under their wings in the wearisome heat of the summer,   575
Then are the goats at their fattest, and wine tastes best at the vintage,
Women are then their most wanton. but men are then very feeble,
Forasmuch Sirius scorches their heads and their knees in his ardor,
Also the skin dries out in the wearisome heat. At that time let
There be the shade of a rock and some wine from the vineyards of   580
    Biblis,[24]
Cakes that are moistened with fresh goat's milk when they're practically
    dried up,
Meat of a heifer that, fed in the woods, has not yet given birth,
Also of newborn kids. It is pleasant to drink of the bright wine,
Sitting at ease in the shade, one's appetite sated with good food,
Turning one's face in the western direction of cool-blowing Zephyr.   585
From the perennial spring that flows crystalline and unsullied,
Pour out three portions of water mixed with a fourth part of neat wine.
Set your domestics to winnow the sacred grain of Demeter,
Grinding it down at the first appearance of mighty Orion[25]
In a well-aerated place and over a well-polished threshing   590
Floor. When you've measured it, carefully put it up in bins built for
    storage.

24. In Thrace or on Naxos, or a varietal; not to be confused with Byblos in Phoenicia.

25. Another constellation, "the hunter," very visible even today.

When you have stored all your goods under lock and key in your own
   house,
Set about hiring a steward with no household of his own, and
Look for a maid with no child; one nursing a brat is a bother.

595 Also take care of the dog with the pointed teeth; don't begrudge him his
   rations,
   Lest any burglar who sleeps by day should purloin your possessions.
   Fodder and litter in plenty provide for your mules and your cattle.
   Afterward, let your domestics unbend their knees, and release your two
      oxen.
   Then when Orion and Sirius enter the center of heaven,
600 And when Arcturus is glimpsed through the roseate fingers of dawn,
   Perses, it's time to snip all the bunches of grapes for the household,
   Spread them outside in the sun ten days and ten nights altogether,
   Cover them over for five days, then on the sixth day extracting
   Into containers the gift of jolly and gay Dionysus.
605 But when the Pleiades set, and the Hyades,[26] also Orion,
   Do not forget it is now full season for plowing and sowing;
   May the good seed tuck snugly and generate under the topsoil.
   If a desire for the comfortless dangers of seafaring grips you,
   After the Pleiades, fleeing the crude, brute strength of Orion,
610 Tumble into the mist-covered sea, beware of the winds then,
   Verily all of them gusting every which way in a tempest,
   Then you should no longer keep ships out on the glistening water.
   Take my advice, just remember that agriculture is safer.
   Pull up your boat on the dry land, fill it with stones mighty tightly
615 On every side, to withstand the force of the wind when it's blowing
   Wetly, and pull out the bilge plug, so the rain may not rot it.
   Tidily stow all your tackle inside your house for the winter;
   Put up the wings, that is, sails, of your seafaring ship very neatly,

26. The "rainy" constellation.

Hang up your well-manufactured rudder to smoke in the fireplace.
See that you wait for the sailing season to make its appearance;   620
Thereupon drag out your swift ship down to sea, and aboard it
Place an appropriate cargo, and you'll sail home with a profit.
So it was, you great idiot Perses, my father and yours took
Ship more than once, as he lacked a respectable living on dry land,
Till on this spot he arrived after crossing the stretches of deep sea,   625
Leaving Aeolean Cyma²⁷ aboard a black vessel in flight from
Neither abundance nor riches nor blessed material plenty,
But that unbearable poverty Zeus has inflicted on humankind.
Our father settled near Helicon²⁸ Mount, in a miserable village,
Ascra: it's horrid in winter, obnoxious in summer, and never   630
Pleasant. So, Perses, remember your tasks, and especially sailing.
Though you admire a small craft, put all your freight in a big one,
Seeing the better the cargo, the better the profit compounded
Surely will be, if the wind holds back its malevolent blasts, and
If you would only convert your ridiculous leanings to commerce,   635
Eager to flee from debt and avoid insalubrious hunger.
Then I shall show you the measure and ways of the bellowing sea,
      though
I am no expert on nautical matters or nautical vessels,
For I have never by ship sailed over the breadth of the broad sea,
Ever, except to Euboea²⁹ from Aulis,³⁰ where the Achaeans   640
Waited all winter through great storms, till they had marshaled the
      people
Out of our own holy Hellas to Troy with its beautiful women.
Thence to the games that commemorate wise Amphidamas³¹ I voyaged,

27. A small town on the northern coast of Asia Minor, or Aeolis.
28. One of the haunts of the Muses, near Ascra, a village that Hesiod put on the map.
29. The long island stretching down the east coast of Greece.
30. The small port on the mainland from which Greeks (Achaeans) embarked for Asia and Troy.
31. A prominent citizen, otherwise unknown, of Chalcis, the capital of Euboea.

Coming at last unto Chalcis's widely advertised contests,
645 Games that the sons of that brave man had there established. I swear I
Bore off the poetry prize, a tripod with wrought-iron handles,
Which I devoted, of course, to the Muses of Helicon—there first
They had apprised me of clear-voiced music and poetry also.
That's the extent of my total acquaintance with nail-studded ships, but
650 Nevertheless, I can tell you the mind of Zeus, who is lord of the aegis,
Seeing the Muses have taught me to sing an incredible poem.
After the fiftieth day that follows the solstice of summer,
After the season of withering heat begins to be over,
That is the right time, Perses, for men to go sailing: you will not
655 Wreck at that season your boat, no seas will make off with your sailors,
Unless Poseidon, the earth shaker, acting with malice aforethought
Or Zeus, who is king of immortals, should want to destroy them:
For in their hands are the equal outcomes of good and of evil.
This is the season when winds are benign, and the sea is not harmful;
660 You can entrust yourself carelessly then to the care of the breezes;
Drag down your ship to the sea, and be sure there is everything on it.
Hurry in order to come as fast as you can to your homeland.
See you don't wait for the new wine, nor for the rains of the autumn,
Nor for the winter that follows the south wind's terrible tempests,
665 Stirring the sea up as they accompany copious rain squalls,
Zeus's autumnal gales that render the deep such a danger.
Spring is another occasion for laboring men to go sailing.
When for the first time leaves that unfold on the top of a fig tree
Look to a man the size of the footprints made by a crow, the
670 Sea then is open, and spring is a suitable season for sailing.
Not that I praise it, indeed; spring isn't my favorite sailing
Season, so snatched at, a time so hard to avoid a disaster.
Yet even then, in their ignorance, men sail, knowing no better,
Forasmuch property means more than life to unfortunate mortals.
675 Yes, it's a terrible thing to die in the midst of the billows.
Take, I beseech you, these matters to heart, as I counsel you, Perses.

Never put all of your livelihood down in the hold of a vessel;
Rather, reserving the bulk, entrust the remainder on shipboard.
It is a terrible thing to meet with disaster at sea, but
Even more terrible still to try overloading your wagon,   680
Breaking your axle in half and spilling and spoiling your cargo.
Measure is best in all matters; always observe due proportion.

Take to your dwelling a woman when you are the right age, not very
Much before thirty but not much later's the right age to marry.
See that she's four years older than puberty; wed in her fifth year.   685
Marry a virgin to teach her all her respectable duties.
Most of all marry a woman who lives in your neighborhood, nearby.
Looking about you, be sure no neighbor makes fun of your marriage.
Surely a man can obtain nothing better at last than a woman
When she is good; if she's bad, there is nothing more thoroughly   690
     tiresome;
Keeping her eye on her dinner, she kippers[32] her husband (however
Strong) without smoke. She will give him a rude and uncomfortable
     old age.

Try to avoid the displeasure and wrath of the blessed immortals.
Do not consider your closest companion the same as a brother,
But if you do so, be sure that you aren't the first one to wrong him.   695
Do not prevaricate just for the sake of inventing a story.
Should he begin the offense with a word or a deed to insult you,
Do not forget to repay him doubly. But if he again will
Offer you friendship and wants to give satisfaction, receive him
Kindly. That man is a wretch who changes one friend for another   700
Any old time; but do not let your visage belie your emotions.
Do not be over hospitable, nor inhospitable neither,

---

32. That is to say, cures him or smokes him; smoking, an age-old method of preserving fish and meat, is the source of this metaphor.

Known as a friend of the wicked, nor as a detractor of good men.
Don't you go taunting a man with his poverty, though it's lamented,
705 Eating away at the heart: it's a gift of the blessed immortals.
Treasure most precious to mankind would be a tongue that is sober,
And the most beautiful pleasure is one enjoyed in proportion.
If you will speak any evil, you'll hear much more pretty quickly.
Do not be churlish and rude at a feast where guests are in plenty.
710 Pleasure is greatest in common, and your expense is much smaller.
Never at sunrise pour a libation of glistening wine to
Zeus or the other immortals with unwashed hands, or the gods will
Not be inclined to your prayers but spit them again in your own face.
One should not urinate facing the sun while standing erect, but
715 One should remember always to do it at sunset and sunrise.
Nor should you piss on the path or next to the path when out walking;
Nor should you do it when naked; nighttime belongs to the blessed.
Either a god-fearing man, wise, knowing, will squat when he pisses,
Or he will go to the inner wall of some fortified courtyard.
720 Don't go exposing your privates bespattered with sperm at the fireside,
Even inside your own house, so shamelessly; rather, avoid this.
When you return from a somewhat lugubrious funeral, do not
Aim to beget any children, but after a festival do it.
Do not cross over on foot the fair-running currents of ever-
725 Rolling rivers before you pray, as you gaze at the lovely
Waters and washing your hands in the clear and delectable liquid.
Someone who crosses a stream without washing his hands will
  encounter
Evil, divine retribution, and all sorts of troubles hereafter.
No one should clip off the dry tip next to the quick on his five-branched
730 Members[33] with glittering iron during the gods' celebrations.
Never position a ladle on top of a mixing bowl at a
Bibulous party; unmerited bad luck follows upon that.

33. An example of metonymy rather than metaphor; cutting the finger- or toenails.

When you are building a house, take care not to leave it unfinished.
Otherwise, raucous crows will be likely to perch on it, cawing.[34]
Don't take food or water for washing with out of a cauldron   735
Hallowed by none of the gods; such pots are extremely unlucky.
Do not permit any twelve-year-old boy to sit on an unmoved
Object: that isn't too good, depriving a male of his manhood;[35]
Nor any twelve-month-old child, for that has a similar outcome.
Do not perform your ablutions in bathwater used by a woman: 740
There is a nasty pollution attaching to that for a long time.
If you should happen upon some sacrifice that is still burning,
Do not make fun of the mystery: heaven takes vengeance on that, too.
Don't ever piss in the outlets of rivers that flow to the sea or
Piss into springs; on the contrary, see you strictly avoid it.   745
Do not relieve yourself therein; it isn't decent to do so.
Act in this way and evade the malicious talk of us humans.
Gossip, moreover, is evil, so light it is easily lifted,
Yet it is terribly painful and awfully hard to get rid of.
Nobody's talk is dispersed altogether as long as a lot of   750
People repeat it, for Gossip herself is some kind of a goddess.

Keeping the days that derive from Zeus in appropriate order,
Kindly inform your domestics about them, specifically that the
Thirtieth day of the month[36] is best for inspecting and handing
Out food. Wherever people correctly determine the truth, then   755
That is the calendar long ordained by the Giver of Counsel.[37]
Foremost, the first and the fourth and the seventh are days that are holy,

34. In many cultures, crows are ominous, particularly of death.

35. Only a speculative anthropologist could begin to explain this and some of the
other ritual dos and don'ts in Hesiod, but they are superstitions of the same sort as not
spilling salt or stepping on a crack—equally inexplicable.

36. Wholly ignorant of the week, Hesiod divided the thirty-day month into three
decades. Thus, "the first ninth" is the ninth day of the first ten-day division, and so
forth. He also counted by the waning and waxing moon.

37. One of the titles of Zeus.

For on the seventh Latona[38] gave birth to Apollo, whose sword is
Gold. Furthermore, both the eighth and the ninth, two days in the final
760 Phase of the waxing moon, are propitious for human endeavors,
And the eleventh as well as the twelfth are alike very good days,
Either for shearing the sheep or for getting a generous crop in,
Though the twelfth day of the month is superior to the eleventh;
That is the day when the airborne spider is spinning her frail web
765 In broad daylight, the day when the shrewd ant garners her heap, and
Women on that day set up their looms to further their weaving.
Shun the thirteenth of the waxing month for beginning your sowing;
That is, however, the best time for setting your plants out,
And though the sixth of the midmonth isn't auspicious for planting,
770 Yet it is good for all male births, not so auspicious for females,
Neither when first they are born nor when they are given in marriage.
Nor in a month is the sixth day fit for the birth of a girl child,
Though it's a perfect occasion for castrating kids and mature rams,
Also a beautiful day for building a fence round a sheep pen.
775 This day favors the birth of a boy, who'll be fond of sarcastic
Talk and of lies and of devious murmurs and sly conversation.
Geld on the eighth of the month your boar and your bellowing bullock,
But on the twelfth you should rather castrate your hardworking donkey.
Then at noon on the glorious twentieth day will a sage be delivered;
780 Anyone born on this day will likely be terribly clever.
Fine is the tenth for the birth of a male, but the fourth of the midmonth
Favors a female. This too is a day to domesticate sheep and
Shambling short-horned cattle, along with a sharp-toothed dog and
Hardworking donkeys. So take them in hand. But beware, should it be the
785 Fourth of the month as it waxes and wanes, for a heartbreaking sorrow
Gnaws at the mind then: a day that is overabundantly fateful.
Bring home blithely your bride on the fourth of the month, but consult
the

38. Latin name of Leto; see index.

Avian omens for what is best in the business of marriage.
Stay off the fifth, which is difficult, terrible, dreary, and painful,
For on the fifth they say that the Furies attended the birth of   790
Oath,[39] who was borne by Discord to make all perjurers suffer.
Following careful inspection, scatter Demeter's devoted
Grain on the well-smoothed area, in the midmonth on the seventh.
Then let the woodcutter cut stout beams for construction of houses,
Many ships' timbers as well, adapted for shipbuilding rightly.   795
But on the fourth of the month undertake the construction of trim
    ships.
The ninth day in the midst of the month will get better at evening,
But the first ninth of the month is perfectly harmless for humans
This is an excellent day for planting the seed and for childbirth,
Whether for females or males; for the day's never totally evil.   800
Few people know that of days of the month twenty-seventh is best for
Opening jars[40] and the yoking of oxen and mules and swift horses,
Also for dragging a swift ship fitted with multiple benches
Down to the glistening sea. Few label this day by its real name.
Open a jar on the fourth in the midst of the month, of all days the   805
Holiest. Not many know that the best time of day of the twenty-
First is the coming of dawn; the evening is not so propitious.
These are the days that are notably profitable to us earthlings;
Others, like dice miscast, are unlucky, productive of nothing.
Everyone praises a different day, but few understand that   810
Sometimes a day is a stepmother, other times more like a mother.
Happy and lucky in days like these is a man understanding
All of these matters, who does his work and displeases no deathless
God, and is learned in bird lore,[41] never committing a trespass.

39. Personification; oaths were, of course, as essential to law then as now.
40. Grain, as well as oil and wine, was stored in jars in the ancient world.
41. Some think that Hesiod here was preparing the transition to a work on ornithomancy, the existence of which ancient opinion denies.

THEOGONY

Let us begin to sing of the Muses of Helicon first, who   1
Have and inhabit their shrine on that large and numinous mountain.
Furthermore, round some spring that is violet-colored, on tender
Feet they are dancing or round the altar of Zeus the almighty,
Bathing their delicate skin in the spring of Permessus or in the   5
Spring of the horse[1] or of sacred Olmeius; they often create their
Lovely and beautiful dances on top of Mount Helicon's summit.
Thence they arise and they go forth wholly enveloped in darkness,
Walking abroad in the night, projecting their beautiful voices,
Singing of Zeus, who sustains the aegis, and reverend Hera,   10
Lady of Argos[2]—wherever she wanders, her sandals are golden—
Hymning the daughter of Zeus, who carries the aegis, Athena
With gray eyes, and Apollo and Artemis, lover of arrows,
Also Poseidon, who holds the earth and occasionally shakes it,
Reverend Themis[3] and coy Aphrodite, who glances askance, too,   15
Beautiful Hebe,[4] whose garland is gold and lovely, Dione,[5]

1. Pegasus, the winged horse from whose hooves many a sacred spring sprang.
Springs are generally sacred to the Muses, who may originally have been water sprites,
nymphs, or naiads.

2. Argos, in the Peloponnesus, was sacred to Hera (Zeus's third wife), as Athens was
to Athena, etc. Most cities had their special, tutelary deity.

3. "Justice" or "Steadfast," Zeus's second wife; a partial personification, like Hebe
(Youth).

4. "Youth," a minor deity; in Homer, the cupbearer of the Gods and heavenly wife of
Heracles.

5. Mother of Aphrodite in some versions.

Leto,[6] Iapetus, also Cronus, whose counsel is crooked,
Dawn, the magnificent Sun, and the Moon, with her radiant visage,
Earth, and the might of the Ocean, and Night, who personifies
    blackness,
20   All of the sacred race of immortals enduring forever.
Such are the goddesses who taught Hesiod beautiful songs once
While he was shepherding lambs in the shadow of Helicon's holy
Mountain, and these were the very first words they uttered to me, those
Nymphs of Olympus, the daughters of Zeus, who carries the aegis.
25   "Wilderness shepherds, ignoble excuses for men, merely bellies.
We are accustomed to tell many lies that resemble the facts, and
We are accustomed to speak, when we wish to, the literal truth, too."
So the articulate daughters of Zeus the magnificent spoke, and
Gave me a staff, a sprout they had plucked of the vigorous laurel:
30   It was a marvelous thing. They inspired me with vocal, prophetic
Song, to enunciate matters to come and others that have been.
Me they commanded to sing of the race of the blessed immortals,
Hymning themselves at beginning and end of every poem.
What is, however, to me all that stuff about oak trees and stones?

35   You, then, let us begin with the Muses who up on Olympus
Pleasure with music the mighty mind of our heavenly father,
Telling of things as they are, as they will be, and were in aforetime,
Blending their voices which flow inexhaustibly sweet from their open
Mouths; then the home of their father, loud-thundering Zeus, is
    delighted.
40   Glad at the delicate, far flung tone of the Muses, the peaks of
Snowy Olympus and all the abodes of the deathless reecho.
Raising aloft their ambrosial voices in song, they extol the
Worshipful race of the gods first, whom at the very beginning
Earth and extensive Heaven gave birth to: the gods were their children,

6. Latona in Latin, mother of Artemis and Apollo.

Givers of good things. Second, they sing about almighty Zeus, the   45
Father of gods and of men, thus beginning and ending their song, for
Zeus is the highest and best of the gods and the greatest in power.
Next, the Olympian Muses, the daughters of Zeus with the aegis,
Pleasure with music the mind of Zeus, who inhabits Olympus,
Singing a song of the races of humans and powerful giants.   50
Them in Pieria Memory, queen of the hills of Eleuther,[7]
After she lay with the father of gods, the descendant of Cronus,
Bore as a respite from woe and a means of forgetting all sorrow.
Zeus, the astute great counselor, slept with Mnemosyne[8] nine nights,
Going up into her blessed bed far from the other immortals.   55
Then, when a year had passed and the round of the seasons was perfect,
After the months dwindled down and the number of days was
     accomplished,
Memory bore nine daughters whose hearts were intent upon music;
All were unanimous also, their spirits remarkably carefree,
At birth little removed from the summit of snowy Olympus.   60
There were their glistening dancing-floors next to their beautiful
     houses.
Near them the Graces as well as Desire had homes in delightful
Comfort. The Muses, projecting their lovely voices from their mouths,
Sing of the customs and noble characters of the immortals.
They, as they went to Olympus, rejoiced in their beautiful voices   65
And their ambrosial melody. Around them the dark earth rang out
Loudly in time to their hymns. Sweet noises arose from their footsteps
As they progressed to their father, who ruled as a monarch in heaven,
Holding the terrible thunderbolt, grasping the glittering lightning.
After he conquered with violence Cronus, his father, he parceled   70
Out each his role to the gods and apportioned their duties and honors.

---

7. "Freetown," on the border of Attica and Boeotia.
8. Mnemosyne and Memory are, of course, one and the same; these first gods, or
Titans, are a curious mix of personifications and cult names.

This was the song of the Muses, who make their homes on Olympus,
Nine of them, daughters engendered of almighty Zeus. And their names
    were
Cleio, Euterpe, and Thalia, also Melpomene, and her
75 Sister Terpsichore, lovely Erato, Polymnia, likewise
Blessed Urania, also Calliope, first of the Muses.[9]
She is a handmaid waiting on reverend princes. If any
One of these heavenly-nurtured princes the daughters of mighty
Zeus should be pleased to regard, on beholding him when he is new-
    born,
80 Over the tongue of that child they distill sweet liquor from heaven,
Out of his mouth flow honey-sweet words. And then all of the people
Look to the same who decides between differing sides with unbending
Righteousness; speaking decisively, firmly, he can in a little
While understandingly put an end even to serious quarrels.
85 This is the function of sensible kings, that whenever the people
Err in assembly, the kings set right the affairs of the people
Easily, talking them over with soft words, gentle persuasion.
Making his way through the throng, he is greeted and cheered like a
    god, with
Honeyed respect, and he stands out always when people assemble.
90 Such is the holy and glorious gift of the Muses to mankind,
For it is thanks to the Muses and to far-darting Apollo
That there are singers and poets on earth and performers on harps; but
Kings are descended from Zeus, who is happy whomever the Muses
Love and befriend, from whose mouth flows speech that is sweeter than
    honey.
95 So, if a person through harboring grief in his freshly bereaved mind
Parches his heart with incessant distress, and a wandering minstrel

9. Literally, more or less, "Fame," "Charm," "Plenty," "Sweet-singer," "Delightful
dancer," "Lovely," "Polyphony," "Heavenly," "Fair-faced"; whether these names were tra-
ditional or Hesiod's invention we cannot, of course, tell, but they sound made up. The
functions of each were not assigned till later.

Serving the Muses then sings of the glorious doings of former
Men and of blessed immortals who hold and inhabit Olympus,
Instantly he will forget disagreeable thoughts and remember
Nothing of sorrow; the gifts of the goddesses swiftly divert him.   100
Hail to the children of Zeus, who give us delectable song and
Publish the holy descent of immortals existing forever,
Those that of old were engendered of Earth and of star-spangled
    Heaven
Or of mysterious Night, even those that were bred by the salt sea.
Tell now how did the gods and the earth first come into being,   105
Rivers as well, and the limitless sea with its storm-driven swells, and
Also the twinkling stars and the widespread heaven above all.
Tell how the gods then divided their wealth and appointed their riches,
How they at first got hold of the heights of wrinkled Olympus.
Tell me of these things, Muses that dwell on the heights of Olympus,   110
From the beginning, and say which first of them came into being.

First of all, Chaos came into existence; thereafter, however,
Broad-bosomed earth took form, the forever immovable seat of
All of the deathless gods who inhabit the heights of Olympus,
And murky Tartarus,[10] tucked in a cleft of extensively traveled   115
Earth; also Eros,[11] most beautiful god among all the immortals,
Loosening limbs, dominating the hearts and the minds and the
    well-laid
Plans both of all the immortals and all of susceptible mankind.
Next, out of Chaos, with Erebus,[12] black Night too was engendered,
And out of Night were the Aether and Daylight together begotten,   120
Whom she conceived after lying with Erebus lovingly, and bore.

10. The underworld; see below, lines 730–40.
11. Love, Cupid in Latin, son of Aphrodite, the abstract son of a primordial mother; causing one to wonder whether such personifications came first or were back-formations from a common verb, as here.
12. Another hell-realm, from an Indo-European root for "darkness."

Earth to begin with engendered her firstborn, star-studded Heaven,
Equal in size to herself, to conceal her on every side, in
Order to furnish a solid foundation for the blessed forever.
125 Next she gave birth to immense, high mountains, the pleasant retreats of
Goddesses, nymphs who inhabit the glens of the mountainous
woodlands.
Also she bore the unfathomable deep with its wind-driven swells, the
Sea, but without the assistance of love or desire; after she had
Slept with Uranus (the Sky), she gave birth to the eddying Ocean,
130 Coios and Creios, Hyperion, Iapetus, Thea and Rhea,
Themis, Mnemosyne, golden-wreathed Phoebe, and lovable Tethys;
Heaven and Earth[13] bore, last of their children, intelligent Cronus,
Their most redoubtable offspring, who hated his vigorous father.

Earth gave birth to the Cyclopses, superabundant in life force,
135 Thunder, Lightning, and Flash, who was powerful and stout hearted,
Furnishing thunder to Zeus, manufacturing thunderbolts for him.
Similar were they in every other respect to the gods,
Save that a singular eye was set in the midst of their foreheads.
Cyclopses were their eponymous nicknames, which is to say, "Round
Eyes,"
140 Seeing a singular circular eye was set in their foreheads.
Physical strength, brute force, and mechanical cunning their works
showed.
Three other sons were engendered by Heaven and Earth, who were very
Mighty and powerful, not to be lightly or frequently mentioned,
Cottus, Briareus, Gyges, unruly and troublesome children,
145 For from their shoulders a hundred hands unattractively sprouted.
Likewise there grew from the shoulders of each fifty heads on their sturdy
Bodies. A strength irresistible went with their awful appearance.

13. Gaia, eldest of beings after Chaos, gave birth to the sky (Uranus) and the sea,
compared to which these Titans are of secondary importance, unless noted elsewhere.

Such were the terrible children begotten by Heaven on Earth and
Loathed from the first by their very own father, who, when they were
    infants,
Tucked them away in a hole in the earth and prevented their coming   150
Up to the light; and Uranus rejoiced in his own evildoing.
Earth, though gigantic, was painfully stuffed on the inside and groaned
    out
Loud. She was quick to develop a scheme both cunning and wicked;
Swiftly creating an element, gray-colored iron, of it she
Fashioned a great big sickle, and said to her dearly loved children,   155
Speaking out boldly, courageously, although afraid in her own heart,
"My dear children, begotten, alas! of a reprobate father,
Listen to me and obey: let us punish your father's wrongdoing;
He was the first to conceive of disgraceful and criminal conduct."
That's what she said. They were all of them frozen by fear, so that no one 160
Uttered a word, until mighty, intelligent Cronus took courage,
And he addressed in the following words his worshipful mother:
"Mother, I would undertake to accomplish this deed, for I haven't
Any respect at all for our wretched, unspeakable father,
Who was the first to conceive such disgraceful and criminal conduct."   165
So he declared, and magnificent Earth was heartily gladdened.
Taking her son by the hand, Earth hid him in ambush, and put a
Serrated scythe in his hand, and disclosed to him wholly her dire plot.
Ushering night in, Uranus visited Gaia,[14] desiring
Amorous intimacy; he extended himself all around and   170
Over the earth, while his son from his ambush protruded his left hand;
Taking the formidable broad serrated blade in his right, he
Hastily cut off his own father's privates and cast them behind him.
Nor did they fly from his hand without profit, for Gaia accepted
All of the blood drops gushing therefrom. When the year was   175
    completed,

14. Heaven and Earth personified, respectively.

Earth gave birth to the Furies as well as the big, strong giants,
Splendid in armor and carrying lances and swords in their large hands,
Also the nymphs that are called after ash trees over the boundless
Earth. So when Cronus had cut off those members with iron, he threw them
180 Straightaway down from the dry land into the tumultuous sea surge,
Where they were carried along on the turbulent surface a long time.
Round the divine flesh rose up a colorless foam, whence a maiden
Grew; who at first by the holy island of Cythera drifted,
Coming at length and at last to the wave-bound island of Cyprus,
185 Where the inspiring and beautiful goddess set foot, and the grass grew
Under her tapering feet, whom immortals and mortals together
Call Aphrodite, because she was born from the spume of the sea, and
Beautifully wreathed Cytherea, since she arrived at Cythera;
Cyprus-engendered, because she was born on the sea-isle of Cyprus;
190 Genital-loving, because she had sprung from sexual organs.
Eros accompanied her; she was followed by comely Desire when
First she was born, and she entered at once the immortals' assembly.
Such were the honors allotted to her from the very beginning.
This was the destined business she played among men and immortals:
195 Maidenly whispers and smiles and giggles and girlish deception,
Pleasure exquisitely pleasant and love that is sweeter than honey.

Mighty Uranus, who was their father, sarcastically named the
Sons he himself had begotten, collectively, "strenuous Titans,"
Saying they'd striven outrageously, strenuously to perform a
200 Terrible deed, one for which they would surely be punished hereafter.

Night also bore reprehensible Doom and her relative, black Fate;[15]
She was delivered of Death and of Sleep and the legions of nightmares.
Afterward pitch-black Night, who'd had intercourse really with no one,

15. Why Fate is a single goddess here and three goddesses just below is unclear; a certain inconsistency must be apparent by now, not only in the genealogies.

Gave birth to bitter Reproach and to Suffering, painful and poignant,
And the Hesperides,[16] who tend beautiful, golden, delicious   205
Apples beyond illustrious Ocean, and fruit-bearing trees, too;
Also she bore the implacable punishing Furies, and three Fates,
Clotho, Lachesis, and Atropos,[17] who at the hour of their birth give
Mankind their personal rations of bad luck and good for their lifetime.
As for the Furies, they prosecute human transgressions, divine, too;   210
Nor do these goddesses ever relinquish their terrible anger
Till they repay with maleficent scrutiny every sinner.
Also deplorable Night bore Nemesis, who is the bane of
Mortals, and then, in succession, Deception as well as Affection;
Likewise, lamentable Old Age bore she, and hard-hearted Conflict.   215
Yet was despicable Conflict the mother of dolorous labor,
Brutish forgetfulness, hunger and pains that reduce one to tears, and
Battles and fights of all kinds, like homicide, manslaughter, murder,
Quarrels and lies, hard words, altercations, disputes, even lawsuits,
Civil disorder, and ruin, which go by their nature together,   220
Finally, Oath, which of all things on earth worst punishes men when
Anyone perjures himself deliberately and is forsworn.

Nereus,[18] true, unforgetful, and honest, was born of the Sea, the
Eldest of all of his children, so sometimes they call him the Old Man,
For he is truthful and gentle and never forgetful of justice,   225
Seeing that all of his knowledge tends toward kindness and healing.
Magical Thaumas[19] and arrogant Phorcys[20] again he engendered,
After he coupled with Earth, in addition to pretty-cheeked Ceto,

16. The daughters of Evening (Hesperus), which is to say, the West; their golden apples were possibly oranges.

17. She who spins, she who distributes, and she who is not to be averted.

18. Grandfather of Achilles; this sea-god wrestled with Heracles, changing shapes and, indeed, substances, from water to fire, etc.

19. The root of his name means "magic" or "marvel," hence the adjective.

20. Father, with his sister Ceto, of, besides the monsters mentioned below, the Sirens and Tritons.

Handsome Eurybia, with an immoveable heart in her bosom.

230 These are the loveliest goddesses ever conceived in the fallow
Sea, and begotten by Nereus, mingled in passion with well-kempt
Doris, the daughter of Ocean, that perfectly circular river:
Ploto, Eucrante, and Sao, together with great Amphitrite,
Kindly Eudora, and Thetis, Galena and Glauce, the gray eyed,

235 And Cymothoe and Speio, and Thoe and Halia, lovely-
Faced Pasithea, Erato, and Eunice whose arms are outstandingly rosy,
Charming Melite and fair Eulimena and gracious Agave,
Doto and Proto and pleasing Pherousa and swift Dynamena,
Nisaea also, Actaea and Protomedea and Doris,

240 And Panopea and gorgeously formed Galatea and rosy-
Armed Hipponoe and sexy and sweet Hippothoe, as well as
Slick Cymodoke, who smooths out the billows and blasts of the goodly
Winds on the fog-covered face of the deep with Cymatolege's
Help and the help of neat-ankled, divine Amphitrite;

245 Cymo and also Eione and beautifully wreathed Alimede,
Plus Glauconome, whose pleasure is laughter, and Pontoporea
And Leagora, Euagora, Leomedea and fair Polynoe,
Lysianassa, Euarne (lovely to look at and wholesome
Naturally) and Psamathe as well with her perfect complexion,

250 Heavenly Menippe, Neso, Eupompe, Themisto, Pronoe,
Lastly Nemertes, whose intellect equals her deathless papa's.
These are the daughters of Nereus, knowledgeable in all good works.
Thaumas was wed to Electra, a daughter of deep-rolling Ocean,
Who was the mother of swift-footed Iris[21] as well as the hairy

255 Harpies, Aello and swift Ocypetes, whose quick-moving wings kept
Up with the blasts of the winds and the birds, flying quickly as time flies.
Ceto delivered to Phorcys the Graiai with beautiful faces,
Who had been gray-haired since birth, so that both the immortals and
    mortal

---

21. Messenger of the gods.

Men who inhabit the whole earth call them "old women" or Graiai,
Violet-garbed Pamphedo, Eyo whose garment is saffron;   260
Also the Gorgons, who dwell far beyond the illustrious ocean
Out on the borders of night with the shrill-voiced daughters of evening,
These being Sthenno, Euryale, and gruesome Medusa, who suffered
Grievously: she was the one who was mortal, the others immortal.
But with Medusa alone black-haired Poseidon would lie in   265
Deep and luxuriant meadows amid all the flowers of springtime.
Later, when Perseus cut off her head, there sprang from her blood great
Chrysaor, also the winged horse Pegasus, namely, the "Spring-Sprung,"
Seeing he sprang from the springs that surround the headwaters of
    ocean.
Chrysaor (Gold Sword)[22] was so called from his grasping a golden   270
Sword. Winged Pegasus, flying away, left behind him the earth, the
Mother of flocks, and approached the immortals and dwells in the
    halls of
Zeus, where he brings that dispenser of council his thunder and
    lightning.
Meanwhile, Chrysaor, having seduced Callirhoe, the daughter of
    far-famed
Ocean, begot fell Geryon, who had three heads on his shoulders,   275
Whom overmuscular Heracles killed on the isle Erytheia[23]
The same day that he drove off his broad-browed, rambling cattle
Even to blessed Tyrins, traversing the fords of the ocean
After he'd murdered the herdsman, Eurytion, also his kinsman
Orthus, who lived in a dim homestead beyond glorious Ocean.   280
Ceto gave birth to another impossible monster resembling

22. Though this etymology is sound, the foregoing is not. Pegasus seems to be a pre-Greek word. A golden sword was also an adjunct of various later divinities and semi-divinities, such as Apollo, Demeter, and Orpheus.

23. It was one of the labors of Hercules, to give him his Latin name, to rustle the cat-tle of this monster, at the bidding of Heracles' stepmother, Hera, whose place in his own name gives rise to conjecture. Tyrins is not far from Argos and Lerna.

Neither in any respect mere mortals or godly immortals,
Deep in a cavernous hole in the earth, strong-minded Echidna;
Half of her looked like a nymph, bright-glancing and fair of
  complexion,
285 Half of her looked like a monstrous serpent, tremendous and dread with
Spots on her skin, who devoured raw flesh in the bowels of blessed
  earth.
There was her cave underneath an immovable hollowed-out boulder,
Far from the regions of men, who are mortal, and gods, who are
  deathless;
There the Olympians gave her a glorious dwelling to live in
290 Under the soil of Arima[24] in watchfulness, gruesome Echidna;
Deathless and ageless that nymph lives all of the days of her lifetime.
And with that bright-eyed maiden there coupled in sexual union,
So it is said, overbearing and lawless and terrible Typhon.[25]
Pregnant, Echidna gave birth to the following murderous children.
295 Orthus was first to be born, fell Geryon's bloodthirsty hound dog.
Second, she bore an indomitable, an unspeakable monster,
Cerberus, eater of raw flesh, Hades'[26] stentorian watchdog.
Cerberus had fifty heads[27] and was insolent, reckless, and mighty.
Third, she gave birth to the Hydra of Lerna,[28] with grisly ideas,
300 Nurtured by white-armed Hera's implacable hatred for strong-armed
Heracles (heir of Amphitryon, by-blow of Zeus),[29] who destroyed the
Beast with his pitiless bronze sword, helped by Iolaus and wily,

---

24. In Italy.

25. Typhoon, the hurricane personified.

26. Note that Hades was a person and not a place.

27. In later literature and art, Cerberus has only three heads.

28. A marsh in the Argolid. We still say "hydra-headed" in memory of this multiple-headed monster.

29. Heracles, the most popular hero of the Greek world, was a Theban by birth. His mother was Alcmene and his father Amphytrion, but heroes were often said to be the sons of Zeus. His celebrated labors included, besides those mentioned, dragging Cerberus up from hell and taking him back.

Warlike Athena. The Hydra gave birth to Chimaera, a great and
Terrible creature, exhaling unquenchable fire, fleet footed,
Strong, who possessed three heads, of which one was a hideous lion's,   305
One was a goat's, and the third was a serpent's, a dangerous dragon,
Lion in front, at the tail end a snake, and a goat in the middle,
Breathing a blast incandescent and blazing of withering fire.
Noble Bellerophon[30] slew the Chimaera with Pegasus's aid.
But then the Hydra, submitting to Orthus, gave birth to the deadly   310
Sphinx, the destruction of Thebes, and the lion that wasted Nemea,[31]
Whom most respectable Hera, the consort of Zeus, educated
For devastating the foothills of Mount Nemea, a pest for
Men, as it preyed on the tribes of mankind who inhabited that land,
Lording it over Apesa and Tretus in hilly Nemea;   315
Nevertheless, the superior strength of great Heracles whipped it.
Finally, Ceto, united in sexual congress with Phorcys,
Brought forth a terrible serpent, which down in the hollows of dark
    earth,
On its titanic perimeter, watches the solid gold apples;
This is the fabulous progeny born to Ceto and Phorcys.   320

Tethys[32] gave birth to the following turbulent rivers by Ocean,
Namely, the Nile and the Alpheius, also the deep Eridanus,
Strymon, Menander, as well as the beautiful streams of the Danube,
Phasis and Rhesus and swift Achelous with its silvery current.
Nessus and Rhodion, deep Haliacmon and swift Heptaporos,   325
Granicus, even Aesopus and equally holy Simois,

30. The many stories about this Corinthian hero include elements from the biblical
Joseph's encounter with Potiphar's wife and the story of Icarus, who also tried to fly to
heaven and failed. His genealogy is laid out in the Iliad (6155 ff). He accomplished his
trials with the aid of the winged horse Pegasus, a gift from Athena.

31. A broad valley on the north of the Argolid; here Heracles performed another of
his labors, slaying a lion sent by Hera.

32. Sister of Ocean, both children of Earth and Heaven.

Peneus. Hermus and mighty Suggaris, smooth-flowing Caicus,
Ladon, Parthenius, placid Ardescus and sacred Scamander.
Tethys gave birth to as well a divine generation of daughters
330 Who, on the earth, with his lordship Apollo as well as the rivers,[33]
Raise up the children of men, a vocation that Zeus has appointed:
Peitho, Admete, Ianthe, Electra and Doris and Prymno,
Heavenly looking Urania, Hippo and Clymene also,
Rhodeia and Callirhoe and Zeuxo and Clytie, Idyia
335 And Pasithoe, Plexaura, Galaxaura and winsome Dione,
Plus Melobosis and Thoe and sweet-to-behold Polydora,
Cerceis, naturally lovable Pluto, and cow-eyed Perseis,
Ianeira, Acaste and Xanthe, Petreia and lovely Menestho,
Also Europa and Metis, as well as Eurynome and, in her yellow
340 Tunic, Telestho, Chriseis and Asia, delightful Calypso,
Also Eudora and Tyche, Amphitro, and foremost of all, Styx.
These are the senior maidens born to the Ocean and Tethys,
But there are plenty of other trim-ankled and comely
Daughters of Ocean who, scattered about everywhere, altogether
345 Service the earth and the deeps of the waters, a glorious goddess's
Children, and such are the other abrupt loud-babbling rivers,
All of whose names it is hard for a man who is mortal to tell, but
Those who inhabit the country surrounding them know them in detail.

Theia, seduced by Hyperion, bore the magnificent Sun and
350 Radiant Moon, also Dawn, who appears to all dwellers on earth and
To the immortals, the gods who inhabit the spaces of heaven.
Lying in conjugal union with Crio, superb Eurybia
Bore to him mighty Astraeus and also magnificent Pallas,
Perses[34] as well, a preeminent sage as compared to all others.

---

33. The central role of rivers, as of Apollo, in the growth of civilization is more obvious than that of these sea nymphs.
34. Not to be confused with Hesiod's brother of the same name.

Eos conceived by Astraeus the strong-willed winds, when the goddess   355
Lay in delight with the god: these were Zephyr, the scouring west wind;
Boreas, rushing and fleet-footed north wind; and Notus, the south
   wind.
Afterward, early-born Eos gave birth to the stars that induct the
Dawn, and the rest of the glittering stars such as garland the heavens.
Styx, eldest daughter of Ocean, from sexual union with Pallas,   360
Bore to him emulous Zelos[35] and trim-ankled, victorious Nike
There in their halls, also Kratos and Bios, or Strength and innate Force,
Glorious children, whose home was not anywhere other than Zeus's,
Having no place and no way save where the divinity led them.
But they are dwelling forever at Zeus the deep thunderer's side, as   365
Styx, their unwithering mother, the daughter of Ocean, decided
On the same day the Olympian star-bright hurler of lightning
Summoned together the holy immortals to mighty Olympus,
Saying if one of the gods were to battle the Titans beside him,
He would not cast him aside from his rights, but that everyone should   370
   keep
All of his previous honors and offices with the immortals.
Further, he said that whoever had gone without honor or office
Under old Cronus would come into honors and offices justly.
Styx the undying was first of the gods in approaching Olympus,
Bringing her children, advised by her wise and affectionate father.   375
Zeus, in his gratitude, honored her, giving her excellent presents,
Making her function to serve as the solemn oath of the great gods,
Making her children for all of their days coinhabitants with him.
Such and in so many words was his promise, which he implemented
Thoroughly. Great is the power he wields, and his kingship is mighty.   380
Phoebe anon entered into the comfortable bed of Coeus,
Where she conceived the result of the love of a god for a goddess.

---

35. Envy personified, like Victory following, and the personifications in the next
line.

Then she gave birth to subfusc-robed Leto, eternally pleasant,
Kind to all men that are mortal and gods who, of course, are immortal,
385 Pleasantest from the beginning, agreeably mild on Olympus.
Next, she gave birth to Asteria, well-named goddess whom Perses
Took home once to his marvelous house to be known as his dear wife.
She, being pregnant, gave birth unto Hecate hellcat, whom highest
Zeus, son of Cronus, esteemed, and he gave her splendiferous presents,
390 Namely, a part of the earth and her share in the fallow seabed;
She has an honorable place also in star-spangled heaven,
And she is glorified most of all by the gods, who are deathless.
So nowadays when one of the earth-dwelling brethren performs the
Beautiful rites in accordance with custom and prays to the gods, he
395 Calls upon Hecate. Full and abundant the honor that follows
Easily him whose prayers the considerate goddess receives well,
For of such as were born of the Earth and the Sky-God, she also
Garnered respect, and, of all, she possesses the lot that is her due.
Zeus, son of Cronus, in nothing abused her and took nothing from her
400 That was in gift to the Titanic gods who came earlier; rather,
She holds, as at first the initial division decided,
And wields her ancient rights on the earth, on the sea, and in heaven;
But yet much more still Zeus presents her in kindness:
Sitting by reverend kings enthroned, she assists them in judgment.
405 To him whom she wants to, she mightily gives good things in
    abundance.
So in the forum of folk, she advances the man whom she favors,
And when for mortal combat men buckle their cuirasses on,
Lo! there is Hecate also, and unto such men as she wishes,
Easily offers victory, loading her servants with honor.
410 Fair is she, likewise, when men contend in their beautiful contests,
For in that instance as well, she is present to honor and profit
One who by strength and by prowess prevails in athletics and will, with
Ease, win first prize and elatedly bring it back home to his parents.
Nobly she stands by the horsemen she favors, and as for the sailors,

Men who work hard on the gray, uncomfortable sea, when 415
Ever they pray unto her and the discordant, earth-moving Sea Lord,
Readily Hecate sends a great haul for their nets, but, should that be her
    pleasure,
Readily takes it away when she wishes as soon as they've seen it.
Also she helps in the barn beside Hermes in feeding the livestock,
Herding the cattle; she droves congregations of wandering goats and 420
Flocks of shambling sheep; if she wishes she may increase them
Or may diminish their number, making a few out of many.
Although Hecate is the unique child born of her mother,
Thereafter she will be honored among all the divine immortals.
Zeus, son of Cronus, appointed her nanny of all mortal children 425
Who with their own eyes thenceforth behold the light of observant
Dawn. She was from the beginning the nurse of these children, and
    therefore
Such were her honors. But Rhea, submitting to Cronus, bore splendid
Offspring: Hestia, also Demeter and Hera, whose sandals are golden,
Powerful, strong-armed Hades, who under the earth makes his 430
    dwelling—
Pitiless his disposition—and smashing and seismic Poseidon,
As well as Zeus, the far planner, father of gods and of humans,
Under the force of whose thunder the wide earth shivers in terror.
These every one great Cronus gobbled down whole as they issued
Each from the womb of their sacred mother to sit on her lap, for 435
Thus he intended that no one else of the children of heaven
Should wield regal authority ever among the immortals.
For he had learned from Earth and from star-spangled Heaven that
    he was
Doomed to be overcome by his very own son, namely Zeus,
Strong as he was, through the wiles of the same, though as yet 440
    unconceived, god.
On this account he mounted no purblind vigil, but watching
Out, he devoured his offspring. Terrible grief possessed Rhea

When she was going to bear Zeus, father of men and immortals;
Then she implored her own dear parents, star-strewn Heaven and
    Earth, to
445 Help her come up with some plan, how she might in secret give birth to
Her dear son, and how devious Cronus might pay retribution
For what he'd done to his father and for ingesting his children.
Thoroughly they understood and obeyed their favorite daughter.
They foretold to her everything that was fated to happen
450 Soon to his majesty Cronus as well as his strong-minded son.
They sent Rhea to Lyctos, in the fertile country of Crete.
When she was ready, she gave birth to the last of her children,
Great Zeus, and her Earth-mother took him from Rhea in broad Crete
To nourish the child and as maternal grandmother rear him.
455 Hastily Earth transported the newborn child through the dark night,
First into Lyctos, where taking the babe in her arms she concealed him
Deep in a high-roofed cave in the sacred earth in the hidden
Hollows beneath the luxuriant forests that clothe Mount Aegeum.
But to the earlier Lord of the gods, the scion of Heaven,
460 Earth proffered a great big rock that was wrapped up in swaddling
Bands, and he grabbed it and shoved it all the way down in his belly.
Nor did he guess in his heart that his son, unhurt and unvanquished,
Had been replaced by that stone, and by force and the strength of his
    hands would
Soon overcome him and take all his honors and rule the immortals.
465 Swiftly thereafter, the strength and the glorious limbs of the new and
Future king were augmented and grew. As the years in their passage
Rolled on, great Cronus, whose counsels are crooked, misled by
Gaia's subtle persuasions, vomited up his own offspring.
First, he brought up the stone, which was the last thing he had
    swallowed:
470 Zeus erected that stone in the midst of the wide-traveled earth at
Pytho, that great, good place, underneath the glens of Parnassus,
Set as a sign thereafter, a marvel to men, who are mortal.

Then he unloosed from their grievous bonds all Cronus's brothers,
Heaven's descendants, whom Cronus his father had thoughtlessly put
    down.
And they remembered their nephew in gratitude for all of his kind   475
    deeds
And in their gratitude gave him the thunder and dazzling lightning
Bolts which prodigious earth had concealed in her innermost parts. So,
Trusting in these dread weapons he rules both immortals and mortals.

Thereafter Iapetus married Clymene, beautiful daughter of Ocean,
Her of the shapely ankles,[36] and led her up their bedroom.   480
Clymene bore to her husband a stout-hearted son named Atlas.
Also she bore him Monoetius, highly respected, as well as
Clever, sharp-witted Prometheus, and Epimetheus, foolish
From the beginning, pernicious, an evil to bread-eating mortals.[37]
He was the first to receive from Zeus the maiden Pandora,   485
Whom he had fashioned. Outrageous Monoetius far-sighted Zeus sent
Down to Erebus, striking him low with an incandescent
Thunderbolt for his unreason and overwhelming presumption.
Atlas upholds the broad heavens by force of necessity at the
Ends of the earth, where he stands tall near the Hesperides, who sing   490
Purely, supporting the sky on his head and his muscular shoulders:
Such was the destiny that wise Zeus decided for Atlas.
He bound devious, wily Prometheus tightly in chains too
Tough to escape from, terrible bonds, and he skewered his middle.
Furthermore, on him he set a long-pinioned eagle to eat his   495
Immortal liver, which grew overnight just as much as that bird with
Tapering wings had eaten during the whole day preceding.

36. The obsession, here and elsewhere, with feminine ankles bespeaks the modesty of women of whom little else could be seen. It conduces also to some compound adjectives, such as "trim-ankled," that are clumsier in English than in Greek.
37. Two characteristics of human beings were stressed in ancient Greek: our mortality and our basic diet.

This big bird the courageous son of tapering-ankled Alcmene,
Heracles, killed, thus freeing Iapetus's son from that evil
500 Pest; on the spot, he released him from all his discomfort and torment,
With the connivance of paramount Zeus, king of Olympus,
So the renown and repute of Heracles, who was a Theban
Born, might increase even more over the generous earth.
Taking account of all this, Zeus honored his glorious son and,
505 Though he was angry indeed, he abated his previous anger
Because Prometheus flaunted the counsels of almighty Zeus.
Men had distinguished themselves from the gods at Mecone
First, when foresightful Prometheus brashly dissected a big ox,
Dishing up servings to each, and seeking to bamboozle smart Zeus.
510 Slyly, in front of the others, he set flesh, also the innards
Rich with the juiciest fat, near the hide, half-hid by the ox's
Belly; to Zeus he served white bones, which by artifice and low
Cunning he dished up disguised in the glistening fat of the bullock.
Then to Prometheus spoke the father of gods and of mankind:
515 "Son of Iapetus, most magnificent of all the princes,
See how invidiously, old son, you divided the servings."
So said thundering Zeus, everlastingly shrewd and all-knowing.
Crookedly scheming Prometheus answered him something as follows;
Slyly he smiled to himself as he thought of his crafty deception.
520 "Zeus, most honored and greatest of gods, whose race is forever,
Take of the pieces whichever the heart in your bosom inclines to."
So he declared as he pondered deceit, but Zeus, whose reflections
Are indestructible, knew and was quick to see through the deception,
And he foresaw in his heart much evil to follow for humans.
525 Taking the white fat up in both hands, Zeus grew very angry;
Anger possessed his mind the minute he noticed the ox's
White bones underneath and discovered Prometheus's crafty deception.
That is the reason the races of humans all over the earth burn
White bones to the blessed immortals on incense-redolent altars.
530 Then Zeus, who gathers the clouds, addressed him in bitter vexation,

"Iapetus's son, over all of the others exceedingly smart and
Knowledgeable, old fellow, you haven't forgotten your cunning!"
Zeus, being angry, spoke thus, with a deathless intention in mind, and,
Ever recalling the trick that was played on him, would not entrust the
Fierce inexhaustible fire to the hands of men, who must perish,   535
Creatures engendered of ash trees, who dwell on the face of the earth.
But Prometheus, Iapetus's brave son, thoroughly fooled him,
For he stole inexhaustible fire, whose blaze can be seen from
Far, in a hollow cane, which offended profoundly the mind of
Zeus, who thunders aloft, and his fond heart grew very angry   540
Seeing the twinkle of fire from afar among men, who are mortal.
Straightaway, Zeus prepared for them evil in place of purloined fire.
Famous Hephaestus,[38] the lame god, molded of water and earth the
Shape of a modest maiden by Zeus's advice and divine will.
Then Athena, the gray-eyed goddess, clad her and dressed her   545
Up in a silvery garment. Over her head she draped a
Finely embroidered veil with her hands, a most marvelous sight; with
Lovely garlands of new-grown wildflowers, Pallas Athena
Crowned her. Also, a garland of gold she put on her head, which
Famous Hephaestus the lame one himself devised with his own hands,   550
Artfully fashioning it as a favor to fatherly Zeus.
On it was wrought much intricate workmanship, wonderful to be
Seen; of the monstrous creatures such as the sea and the dry land
Nourish, he put many on it—so radiant beauty and splendor
Shone from it—creatures so lifelike one might suppose they had voices.   555
So when Hephaestus had made this beautiful bane in exchange for
Good, he conducted her to that place where the humans and gods were,
All tricked out by the gray-eyed daughter of powerful Zeus.
Wonderment seized the immortal gods and men who are mortal
When they beheld such a sheer deception and hardship for mankind;   560
But from her are descended untold generations of women.

38. Vulcan in Latin.

And from her you may trace the descent of the pestilent races of
 women;
Dwelling among mortal men, they occasion us plenty of trouble,
Bearing with us in prosperity, never in miserable hardship.
565 Likewise, in beetling beehives bees feed mischievous drones, for
Daily and all day long until sundown, while honeybees labor
Building the white wax honeycombs, drones on the other hand stay at
Home in the sheltering hive and gobble the labor of others.
Similarly did Zeus, who thunders aloft, create women,
570 Bad for mankind, in cahoots in all manner of tiresome mischief.
And he provided another bad thing in exchange for a good thing.
If, to avoid getting wed and the vexing behavior of women,
One doesn't go in for marriage, he arrives at lamentable old age
Lacking somebody to tend to him when he is old, and though he lacks
575 Nothing to live on when he is alive, at his death his relations,
Heirs to a vacant estate, will apportion his substance among them.
Yet on the other hand, for one who chooses the chances of marriage,
To have and to hold a respectable wife in accord with his wishes
From the beginning and through all his days, good squabbles with bad;
 for
580 Any who finds his children unruly will certainly lead a
Life of incessant heartache: that's an incurable evil.
Thus it is possible neither to fool Zeus nor circumvent his
Wits, for not even Prometheus, Iapetus's son, although clever,
Could quite get himself out from the yoke of his heavy displeasure,
585 But necessarily, smart though he was, strong bondage repressed him.
So at the first when their father was angry with stout Briareus,
Cottus, and Gyges, he bound them in strong, irrefrangible bondage;
Being resentful at heart of their mettlesome manliness, beauty,
Also their great size, Uranus banished them under the broad earth;
590 There underground they abode in much torment, discomfort, and
 anguish,
Stuck at the ends of the earth, at the ultimate limits of great earth,

Bitter at heart for a long while, suffering grievous affliction.
These did the offspring of Cronus, as well as the other immortal
Gods whom Rhea, the well-coiffed, bore in conjunction with Cronus,
Bring up again into daylight at the advisement of Earth, for   595
She explained everything thoroughly to them, how with the help of
Uranus's sons they would win bright victory such as they prayed for.
For the Titanic immortals and those begotten by Cronus
Long had been struggling against each other in fierce internecine
Combat, exerting themselves together in heart-wrenching effort,   600
On one side the illustrious Titans from lofty Mount Othrys[39]
And on the other the gods from Olympus, the givers of good things,
Those whom Rhea the fair-haired bore after sleeping with Cronus.
So at that time they were fighting continually with each other
Ten full years as they nursed in their guts indigestible anger.   605
Nor was there any solution or end to the difficult conflict
For either side, but the outcome of battle was equally balanced.
But when Zeus, in the meanwhile, had furnished his monsters with all
     things
Suitable, nectar as well as ambrosia, foods that the gods eat,
Then did the manly spirit of all three swell in their bosoms.   610
When they had eaten their fill of delicious ambrosia and of
Nectar, then Zeus, the begetter of gods and of humans, addressed them:
"Listen to me, you glorious children of Earth and of Heaven,
So I may say those things that the heart in my bosom commands me.
Every day for a long time now have we offspring of Cronus   615
Vied with the Titans for power and victory, fighting each other.
Show, for your own part, maintain your immense strength and resistless
Arms in opposing the Titans in bitter, lugubrious battle,
Mindful of all our considerate kindness: haven't you come back
Up to the light after what you endured in uncomfortable bondage   620
Under the mist-filled darkness, all through our inscrutable plans?"

39. In Thessaly; see map.

So he declared, and in answer excellent Cottus responded.
"Sir, you reveal to us nothing we aren't aware of already.
Well do we know your intelligence, also your high understanding;
625 You have become the defender of all the immortals from cold war.
For it is thanks to your thoughtfulness we have returned back again from
Out of the mist-filled darkness and out of our merciless bondage,
Having experienced things unhoped for, O lord, son of Cronus!
So, with inflexible purpose and after considerate planning,
630 We shall assist your all-powerful might in this terrible battle,
Struggling against all those Titans in strong-armed personal duels."
That was his speech, and the deities, givers of bounty, commended
What he had said when they'd heard him. Their spirit was keener for warfare
Than in the past, and they roused themselves up to regrettable battle
635 That very day, every one of them, females and males all together,
Both all the gods called Titans and those who descended from Cronus,
Also the monsters whom Zeus brought up to the light from Erebus
Under the earth, fierce, fearsome, and strong, irresistibly well armed,
For from the shoulders of all of them equally sprouted a hundred
640 Hands; from the shoulders of each of these creatures as well grew fifty
Heads in a similar manner on top of their powerful bodies.
These, as they stood up against the Titans in furious face-off,
Grasped in their powerful hands unwieldy, precipitous boulders,
And on the other hand, meanwhile, the Titans in zeal reinforced their
645 Ranks, so both the opponents displayed their physical strength and
Manual labor. The limitless ocean resounded about them,
And earth crashed in a spasm, the wide sky groaned and was shaken;
Even the heights of Olympus quaked to their very foundations
Under the force of the charge of the deathless immortals, the heavy
650 Shock of whose trampling feet reached even to Tartarus, with the
High thrilling cries of unspeakable onslaught and clanging of heavy
Blows as they hurled at each other their grievous, lamentable missiles.

Then did the noise of their voices when shouting arise to the starry
Heavens; they rushed all together with battle cries loudly resounding.
Neither did Zeus restrain any longer his strength, but his mind now   655
Forthwith was filled with the sense of his might, and he showed forth
   his power,
All of it, all at one time; from Olympus as well as from heaven,
Constantly hurling his lightning, he strode along so that the thunder
Bolts flew thick and fast from his muscular hand, intermingled
Thunder and lightning together, both whirling around in a sacred   660
Burning; the life-giving earth shook on all sides as it kindled
Ablaze, and the huge wood rattled and crashed in the great fire;
All of the land boiled over as well as the waters of Ocean
And the unharvested sea. Hot vapors enveloped the earth-born
Titans; unchecked combustion invaded the radiant upper   665
Air, and the brilliant and glittering glare of the thunder and lightning
Dazzled them, strong though they were, temporarily blinding their eyes.
Then the miraculous fiery heat reached down into Chaos.
It was as if one watched with his eyes and heard with his ears the
Earth and the heavens above it collapsing on top of each other: 670
Such the great thud that would rise if the heavens were falling and
   from the
Earth that they fell on as came from the strife of the gods in collision.
With this the winds brought gravelly earthquake and stifling
   windstorm,
Thunder and lightning, and also the glistening thunderbolt, weapons
Of great Zeus, as they carried the noise and the shouts of the battle   675
Into the midst of both camps. A gargantuan racket arose of
Terrible strife, and the strength of their bellicose arms was apparent
Even as fighting declined; but before that they held one another
Off as they fought without ceasing in vigorous, fierce, single combats.
Then Briareus and Cottus and Gyges, unwearied with battle,   680
First in the forefront, engaged in insatiate, bitterest fighting,
Sending one after another three hundred rocks from their strong hands

To overshadow the Titans with missiles; they sent them beneath the
Widely trod earth, and they bound them with troublesome bonds,
   having conquered
685 Them with their hands in despite of the Titans' arrogant spirit,
Under the earth just as far as the heavens are over the earth, for
Such is the distance from earth into nebulous Tartarus. A bronze
Anvil that fell from the sky for ten nights and ten days on the tenth
   would
Come to the earth, and once more a bronze anvil that fell from the
   earth to
690 Tartarus for ten nights and ten days would arrive on the tenth day.
All about Tartarus marches a bronze palisade, and around the
Neck of it night extends in threefold layers; above it
Flourish the roots of the earth and the sea, which forever is fallow.
There the Titanic divinities under that nebulous darkness
695 Welter, concealed in a place that is foul, at the ends of the huge earth
All through the far-sighted plans of Zeus, who marshals the storm
   clouds.
There is no exit for them, for Poseidon has fitted there doors of
Bronze, and a wall which extends all along on both sides of the doorway.
Also magnanimous Briareus and Cottus and Gyges
700 Live there, the trusty defenders of Zeus, who is lord of the aegis.
There in a row all in order the ultimate sources and limits
Stand, of the darkling earth and of nebulous Tartarus, also
Of the unharvested sea as well as the star-studded heavens,
Loathsome, malodorous, foul—and indeed the immortals detest them.
705 Vast is that chasm, and nobody could, if a year were completed,
Get through it all after first having entered its gateway, for cruel
Wind upon wind would transport him cruelly hither and thither.
This is a fearful and marvelous thing to the deities even.
There stands the awful home of black Night, enveloped in blue clouds.
710 Standing in front of its doorway, the son of Iapetus, Atlas,

Holds on his head and his hands, unfatigued and immobile, the wide
    sky,
Even where Night and Day as they pass one another salute each
Other on crossing the great bronze threshold; while one is descending
Into their dwelling, the other is going abroad through the doorway,
Nor does that mansion at any one time entertain them together.   715
One of them always is out of the house as she passes above the
Earth, while the other abides in the home where she stays to await the
Hour of departure, whenever it comes; and when one of them holds the
Light that illumines all people who dwell on the earth, the
Other, lamentable Night, enveloped in nebulous darkness,   720
Holds in mysterious arms that Sleep which is brother to Death.
That is the place where the children of black Night have their
    apartments,
Namely, Sleep and Death, who are awful divinities, and the
Radiant sun never gazes upon them with glittering sunbeams
As he ascends into heaven and as he descends from the heavens;   725
Of these, the former meanders across the wide earth and the
    broad-backed
Sea and is peaceful and pleasant to men, but the other one's heart is
Iron, his character pitiless, harder than bronze, for whichever
Human he catches he grasps, and he's hateful to all the immortals.
Furthermore, there the reverberant halls of the god of the nether   730
World, strong, powerful Hades, and dreadful Persephone, his queen,
Stand, and a fearful and pitiless watchdog guards them in front. That
Hound has a wicked trick, for he fawns with his tail and his ears on
Those going in, but he doesn't permit anybody to go out.
Watching, he catches and eats anyone going out by the gateway.   735
There is the dwelling as well of the goddess abhorred by immortals,
Terrible Styx, the most senior daughter of retrograde Ocean.
Far from the gods, she inhabits a glorious house overhung by
Sizable rocks, and with silvery columns surrounding it all, it

740 Rises right up to the sky. Not too often the daughter of Thaumas,
 Swift-footed Iris, traverses the broad-backed sea to deliver
 There any message. However, when discord and quarrels among the
 Deathless are stirred up, Zeus sends Iris to fetch in a golden
 Pitcher the gods' great oath from afar, the notorious, chilly
745 Stygian water that trickles down from precipitous heights.
 Flowing a long way under the wide-traveled earth from the sacred
 River, a branch of the Ocean cascades through the blackness of night. A
 Tenth of the waters of Ocean belong to the Styx as her birthright.
 Swirling in nine silver eddies, the stream that encircles the earth and
750 Broad-backed sea falls into the briny, but this one alone, which
 Springs from a rock in the sight of the gods, is a major misfortune.
 One of the gods who inhabit the snow-covered peaks of Olympus,
 When he has poured a libation to Styx, if he perjures himself, lies
 Breathless and doesn't draw breath till the whole of a year is completed.
755 Nor does he ever approach to partake of ambrosia or of
 Nectar, but lies without spirit or voice on a bed that is spread with
 Bedclothes; and him a malignant and magical slumber envelops.
 Once he has done with that illness and come to the end of a long year,
 After that trial, another and harder one follows, one fast on another;
760 For from the gods, whose life is eternal, he's sundered for nine years,
 Never to mix in their councils nor join in theirs feasts for the whole nine
 Years. In the tenth he rejoins the assemblies of all the immortal
 Gods on Olympus. So such is the oath that they swear by the ancient,
 Ageless, primordial water of Styx, and it springs from a hard place.
765 There in a row all in order the ultimate sources and limits
 Stand, of the darkling earth and of nebulous Tartarus, also
 Of the unharvested sea as well as the star-studded heavens,
 Loathsome, malodorous, foul—and indeed the immortals detest them.
 There are the glistening gates and the threshold of natural bronze set
770 Fast and immovable, fixed to continuous, rooted foundations.
 Outside and beyond these, apart from the other divinities, dwell the
 Titans over against inarticulate Chaos; however,

Cottus and Gyges, the glorious allies of stentorian Z

House in the depths of the ocean. However, Poseidon,

Thundering earth-quaker, made Briareus, because he wa

Son-in-law, giving him Cympolea, his daughter, in marriage   805

Then, after Zeus had expelled the Titans from heaven, prodigious

Earth gave birth to the last of her children, Typhoeus, enduring

Sexual union with Tartarus, prompted by gold Aphrodite.

Strong were his hands in defense and in all his endeavors, his feet were

Strong and unwearying, those of a robust divinity. From his

Shoulders a hundred serpentine heads like a terrible dragon's

Sprouted with pitchy, flickering tongues; from the eyes underneath the

Brows in these magical heads, a malevolent fire coruscated.

From all these heads, as he glared all about him, a fire was blazing,   785

And there were voices inside these terrible heads which projected

Every sort of unspeakable voice, for at one time they uttered

Speech such as gods understand, and at others the sound of a loudly

Bellowing bull in the pride of unbridled ferocity; then once

More he would roar like a lion of impudent courage, then whimper   790

Puppylike, wondrous to hear, then hiss till the high hills resounded.

Then would a deed beyond any recourse have been done on that same
    day,

And this Typhoeus would surely have ruled the immortals and mortals

Had not the father of gods and of men been sharp to take notice.

Mightily, harshly he thundered, so loud that the earth all around shook,   795

Making a terrible noise, like the far-reaching heavens above, the

Sea and the streams of the ocean, the pits of the underworld also.

Mighty Olympus unsteadily tottered beneath the immortal

Feet of its lord in arousal, and earth sympathetically groaned. The

Heat that emitted from both of them seized on the violet-hued sea,   800

Blazes of thunder and lightning as well as the fire from the monster's

Burning, the hurricane winds and the thunderbolts' sizzle and crackle.

All of the earth boiled up, and the sky and the sea in addition.

ound and about all the headlands and beaches the breakers were
     crashing
Under the charge of the gods; there occurred an unquenchable
     earthquake.
Hades, who governs the dead in his underworld kingdom, was
     frightened,
So were the Titans, who dwell under Tartarus, round about Cronus,
By that unquenchable racket and horrible clangor of battle.
Zeus, when he'd gathered his strength and taken hold of his weapons,
810 Thunder and lightning contained in a bright-burning thunderbolt,
     leaping
Down from Olympus impulsively, struck at Typhoeus and set on
Fire all the marvelous heads of the monster that sprouted all over
Him. Then, when Zeus had subdued him and whipped him again and
     again with
Lashes of lightning, he hurled him down, crippled; the monstrous earth
     groaned.
815 Flames shot out of the thunderstruck deity where he'd been stricken
Down to the earth in the rough, inaccessible dells of the mountain.
Much of the monstrous earth was dissolved by that weird exhalation,
Melting like tin that is heated by technical means by some sturdy
Workmen in pervious crucibles, or like iron, the strongest
820 Element, tamed and refined by a hot-burning fire in the mountain
Dales, which is smelted in godly earth by the might of Hephaestus.
So earth melted at once in a flash of that blazing and glistening fire.
Into broad Tartarus Zeus, being angered, ejected Typhoeus.
And from Typhoeus arises the force of the humidly blowing
825 Winds, except Notus and Boreas and wholesome, brightening Zephyr,
Winds that are born of the gods, a magnificent blessing for humans.
Every which way and at random those other winds blow on the sea and,
Fitfully rising and falling, descend on the cloud-covered deep, a
Terrible trial for men with their boisterous, roistering breezes;
830 Blowing in different directions at different seasons, they scatter

Vessels and murder their mariners. There is no help for such ills for
Seafaring men who encounter breezes like these on the deep sea.
Furthermore, raging all over the limitless, flowery earth, they
Ruin the beautiful works of mankind, who are earth-generated,
Filling their fields and their dwellings with dust and a horrible uproar.   835
Then at last, when the blessed divinities finished their labor,
Having decided by force their rights in regard to the Titans,
Then they invited Olympian, wide-eyed Zeus to become the
Ruler and king of the gods, as advised by the earth goddess, Gaia.
That being settled, he split their prerogative honors among them.   840
Zeus, being king, first married the goddess of practical reason,
Metis, the wisest, most knowledgeable of immortals or mortals.
But, just as she was about to give birth to gray-eyed Athena,
Zeus, at that moment misleading her wits by a cunning deception
And with his flattering arguments, swallowed her into his stomach,   845
At the advice of the earth goddess, Gaia, and star-studded Heaven.
For they instructed him thusly, in order that none of the other
Gods whose race is eternal should get royal power but Zeus.
All too intelligent children were destined to come out of Metis;
First was the gray-eyed maiden Athena, called Tritogeneia,[40]   850
Who, in intelligent counsel and forcefulness, equals her father.
Afterward, Metis was going to bear him a son of a reckless
Character, larger than life, future king of the gods and of men, too;
But Zeus, before she could do so, swallowed her into his belly,
So that the goddess might teach him the meaning of good and of evil.   855
Second, he wed brilliant Themis, the goddess of law and tradition,
Who bore him the Hours and Eunomia, Dike, and fruitful Irene—
Order and Justice and Peace—regulating the works of us mortals,
Also the Fates, whom considerate Zeus paid the greatest respect to:
Clotho, Lachesis, and Atropos, giver of men's good and evil.   860

40. Various fanciful, geographical explanations are given for this stock epithet of
Athena, but the most likely seems to derive it from an Aeolic word meaning "bo
the head."

Next did Eurynome, she who possessed a surpassingly pretty,
Lovely appearance, the daughter of Ocean, bear the three Graces,
Namely, Aglaia, as well as Euphrosyne, Thalia also.
Graceful indeed, for, from under their eyelids, love—which undoes the
865 Limbs—drips; under their eyebrows, beauty entrancingly glances.
Next Zeus went to the bed of Demeter, who nourishes many,
Who gave birth to Persephone with her white arms, whom Hades
Snatched from her mother; and Zeus, in his wisdom, gave her to Hades.
And yet again to exquisite Mnemosyne—Memory—Zeus made
870 Love, and from her the nine Muses with golden tiaras were born; to
Them festive banquets are pleasing, as well as the pleasure of music.
Leto, uniting in fondness with Zeus, who is Lord of the aegis,
Bore him far-shooting Apollo and Artemis, shooter of arrows,
Lovely, desirable children above all the offspring of heaven.
875 Finally, Zeus made Hera his beautiful, flourishing consort;
Hebe and Ares[41] she bore and Eileithyia, goddess of childbirth,
After uniting in love with the king of the gods and of humankind.
All by himself, from his head, Zeus fathered gray-eyed Athena,
Terrible rouser to battle and leader of armies, that tireless
880 Lady whose pleasure is ever in war cries and warfare and fighting.
Hera engendered the craftsman Hephaestus, not having engaged in
Marital intercourse, for she had quarreled, annoyed with her
     husband—   .
Famous Hephaestus, surpassing in handwork all the immortals.
From Amphitrite and noisy Poseidon, the maker of earthquakes,
885 Mighty, loud-trumpeting Triton was born, who inhabits the sea depths,
Where, with the mother he loves and his lordly progenitor, in a
Mansion of gold he abides, and an awesome divinity he is!
But Aphrodite, in union with shield-breaking Ares, gave birth to
Terror and Dread, those terrible ones who dissipate human
890 Battle formations in cold-blooded war with the sacker of cities,

41. Mars in Latin, the god of war.

Ares, Harmonia also, whom high-minded Cadmus espoused.
Maia, Atlas's daughter, bore Zeus glorious Hermes,
Herald of blessed immortals, having got into his blest bed.
Semele, daughter of Cadmus, having united in love with
Zeus, gave birth to a splendid son, Dionysus, the cheerful   895
God, an immortal though she was a mortal; but now they are both gods.
Also Alcmene, uniting in sexual congress with Zeus, who
Gathers the clouds, bore powerful, muscular Heracles to him.
Furthermore, famous Hephaestus, the splay-footed craftsman,
    espoused the
Youngest of Graces, Aglaia, and made her his blossoming wife.   900
And golden-locked Dionysus espoused fair-haired Ariadne,
Daughter of Minos of Crete, and he made her his blossoming wife.
For him, the scion of Cronus made her immortal and ageless.
Heracles, virile and valiant son of trim-ankled Alcmene,
When he had finished his tiresome trials, took as his blooming   905
Wife upon snowy Olympus Hebe, the child of almighty
Zeus and of Hera, whose sandals are golden; and blessed he is who,
Having accomplished his great undertaking among the immortals,
Lives beyond all human suffering, ageless for all of his days.
Perseis, well-known and beauteous daughter of Ocean, presented   910
The inexhaustible Sun with Aeetes, the monarch, and Circe.[42]
Kingly Aeetes, the son of the sun, who illuminates mankind
Married Idyia, whose cheeks were so fair, to fulfill the divine scheme,
Maidenly daughter of Ocean, the perfect and ultimate river.
She in her turn bore Medea,[43] whose ankles were trim after being   915
Subject to sexual love by the working of gold Aphrodite.

Now farewell to all you who inhabit the halls of Olympus,
Islands and continents, too, and the salt sea between and among them!

---

42. Enchantress and priestess in Odyssey, book 10.
43. Also a witch, heroine of the Argonautica and a play by Euripides.

Sing of the races of goddesses now, and the sweet-spoken Muses,
920 Daughters conceived on Olympus by Zeus, who is lord of the aegis,
Who, when they bedded with men who were mortal, although they
themselves were
Deathless, conceived and brought forth mortal children resembling the
gods.
Goddess of goddesses, queenly Demeter, gave birth to the noble
Demigod Plutus (or Wealth) after lying in love in a fallow
925 Field that had thrice been plowed with heroic Iasion[44] in the
Fertile and prosperous country of Crete. A goodly divinity, Plutus
Travels all over the earth and the broad-backed sea, and to one who
Has the good fortune to find him and into whose hands he may fall,
Plutus gives plenty of money and makes him a prosperous man.
930 Daughter of gold Aphrodite, Harmonia brought forth for Cadmus[45]
Ino and Semele, also the naiad, sweet-cheeked Agave,
Plus Autonoe, who wedded long-haired Aristaeus and bore him
Prince Polydorus in Thebes all encircled with ramparts and towers.
Also a daughter of Ocean, the nymph Callirhoe, in loving
935 Union with strong-willed Chrysaor, obeying the will of the splendid
Goddess of love, Aphrodite, gave birth to the strongest of mankind,
Geryon, whom stout Heracles killed on account of some round-hoofed
Cattle that Heracles stole on the sea-bound isle Erytheia.
Eos[46] bore to Tithonus a son, bronze-helmeted Memnon,
940 King of the black Ethiopians, lordly Emathion also.
Also, by Cephalus Eos engendered a glorious son, strong
Phaethon, who was a man who resembled the gods, and when he was
Only a youngster possessing the delicate blossom of splendid

---

44. Short-lived and insignificant, like most mortal consorts; see Odyssey, book 5,
125ff.
45. Credited with the introduction of writing in Greece and founder of Thebes,
whose later history is too complex to recount here.
46. The dawn, Aurora in Latin, who granted eternal life to her lover, Tithonus, who
forgot to ask for eternal youth also and became a cicada.

Boyhood, no more than a child with a childlike intelligence, smiling,
Lewd Aphrodite enraptured and raped him and made him a temple   945
Night watchman, deep in her holiest temple, a guardian spirit.
Jason the son of Aeson abducted the daughter of royal,
High-bred Aeetes, fulfilling the will of the gods, from Aeetes,
After performing the many and tiresome labors imposed by
Great king Pelias, that overbearing and arrogant, ruthless,   950
Vile evildoer. When Jason had finished these feats, he arrived,
After much toil, at Iolcus, and with him he brought on his swift ship
Roguish Medea, the daughter of royal Aeetes. In wifely
Duty to Jason, the shepherd and king of his people, she bore him
Little Medeus, whom Chiron, the centaur, the son of Phillyra,   955
Reared in the mountains. And so was accomplished the purpose of
   great Zeus.
As for the daughters of Nereus, called the old man of the sea,
Psamathe, queen among goddesses, bore from her love for Aeacus,
Prompted by bright Aphrodite, Phocus; and silvery-footed
Thetis gave birth to Achilles, the lion-heart, breaker of men.   960
And Aphrodite, the gorgeously garlanded goddess of love, in
Union with virile Anchises, bore him heroic Aeneas
High on the summit of wooded, wrinkled, and windswept Mount Ida.
Circe, the daughter of Helios, son of Hyperion, had from
Sexual congress with clever and patient Odysseus offspring,   965
Agrius; also unblemished, impeccable, sturdy Latinus;
And Telegonus as well, via aureate Aphrodite.
Over the far-famed Tyrrhenians all tucked away in the holy
Islands they rule. But Calypso, that lady divinity, being
Mixed up in sexual love with Odysseus, bore Nausithous.   970
These are the goddesses who, while immortal, consorted with mortal
Men and conceived and brought forth mortal children resembling the
   gods.
Now, about womankind sing, sweet-voiced Olympian Muses,
Daughters of almighty Zeus, who is master and lord of the aegis.

THE
HOMERIC HYMNS

THE BATTLE OF THE
FROGS AND THE MICE

TRANSLATOR'S NOTE

In this version of what might be called the "Rhapsodies and Prefaces of the Sons of Homer," I have imitated the meter and diction of the original, in an attempt to give some taste of the peculiar flavor of these hymns, which seem at once solemn and facetious, gay and grand. My dactylic hexameters I allow to contain more undiluted dactyls than the Greek; the lines are, with few exceptions, purely dactylic through the fifth foot; the sixth foot is more often trochaic than spondaic, as the rules of classical scansion would approve. The reason for the predominance of dactyls lies in the accentual character of the English language, where spondees are few and three stressed syllables (as must arise in the case of a spondee followed by a dactyl), almost unheard of. The effect here, though more monotonous, is lighter than that of the original and at least avoids those confusing hiatuses that result from any attempt to write true classical hexameters in English. So powerful has the dactylic rhythm proved, in fact, that I have taken liberties with the accents of certain words for prosodic reasons, much as a composer might set the occasional syllable in such a way as to outrage its spoken pattern while preserving his tune. Thus, while "immortal" and "undying" are accented on the penult, both seem to me defensibly to scan as dactyls because of the audible length of the first foot. Readers are not to quibble at syllables if they hear throughout the steady measure of the hexameter.

   The diction of the *Homeric Hymns* presents as many problems in English as it does in Greek. Composed, at a most conservative estimate, over a period of a thousand years—from 600 BC to AD 400—these lays and invocations in the Homeric style are, like all classical poetry, often deliberately archaic and almost invariably precious. Of great lexicographical interest, they present many odd and out of the way usages and abound, as their frequent citations in Liddell and Scott's Greek dictionary show, in *hapax legomena*. My rule has been to follow the sense, and sometimes the sound, of the Greek as closely as possible, letting archaisms and colloqui-alisms equally intrude when they seemed called for or inevitable, but avoiding an unduly up-to-date contemporary style. The bards who composed these songs for recitation were, despite their beards and their beggary, no Beats; they are, rather, our—as they were Chapman's and Shelley's and the Greeks'—chief instructors in classical language and lit-erature.

I have not invariably reproduced in position the celebrated formulary epithets and phrases so typical of this once oral poetry, and I have, from a strict constructionist's point of view, culpably, even whimsically, varied the translation of any given stock expression. The modern ear and, what is more important, the modern eye like variety; so *hekatabolos*, the most common title of Apollo, becomes in turn "long-distance archer," "accu-rate marksman," "Guard from afar." Yet I trust that enough of the repeti-tive, comfortable character of the original recitation persists to give all but bronze age purists an adequate impression of the incantatory, formal quality of the hymns: "Ah, humankind must endure all the gifts of the gods, though we suffer!"

Finally, it has been my aim to capture also the different tones of voice of the divine protagonists and the idiosyncratic styles of the various hymns. Thus, the *Hymn to Demeter* (II) has a plainness which, in the *Hymn to Pythian Apollo* (III) degenerates into pomposity, as the slyness of *To Aphrodite* (V) explodes into the slapstick of *To Hermes* (IV).

I have preserved the arrangement of the hymns in their classical or-der, that of most manuscripts and editions, for want of a better. This or-der would appear to be roughly chronological according to some theory of date of composition. Hymns I, II, and III certainly seem older, rougher, and more "authentic," while XXX, XXXI, and XXXII seem mod-ern to the point of triviality. An accident of this arrangement is that the longer, narrative hymns (II, III, IV, and V), the major hymns which any-one at all familiar with minor Homerica has read, come first, while the frequently charming, slighter, and later hymns, VIII through XXXIII, are relegated by most readers to neglect. The only obvious alternative was to arrange the poems alphabetically, according to deity, as a sort of Olympian directory, or pantheon, from Aphrodite to Zeus. This too had its drawbacks, notably an air of frivolity; if the present arrangement seems arbitrary, it has at least the sanction of tradition, and like the anonymous authors of these lyrics, I have preferred the familiar, as a rule, to the newfangled and faddish. But I would encourage readers to take the *Homeric Hymns* in any order that they please, as I did in translating them, not following the sequence as set forth here, but beginning and ending where they like.

A burlesque rather than a serious parody or *imitatio Iliadis*, the *Batrachomyomachia* (or *The Battle of the Frogs and the Mice*) is—like the hymns, which it resembles at least in meter—of profoundly uncertain date and authorship, the guesswork of Byzantine grammarians notwithstanding. This comic epyllion belongs, in all but specific mock-heroic reference, to a different literary genre, that of Aristophanes and Aesop, comedy and fable. Unlike the inimitable *Homeric Hymns*, it has been much imitated, as by Vergil in his (?) *Culex*, and Henryson in his *Taill of the Paddok and the Mous*; Rabelais remembers it in *La guerre des andouillettes*, and the *Rape of the Lock* and *Animal Farm* are equally indebted to this anonymous progenitor. Broad in tone, zoomorphic in cast, *The Battle* is a takeoff on the attitudes and epithets of Homeric heroism as seen by a later, softer age. It makes the Olympian deities not merely human but all too human—peevish, ineffectual, and neurotic to a degree unexampled even in the *Iliad*—and far from their aspect in the hymns, in even the latest of which the gods are treated with a real, if at times tender or amused, awe.

Lucian almost might have perpetrated this poem. Its interest for the translator lay in the challenge presented by the ridiculous but apt names of the protagonists and the slapstick battle scenes. Its appeal for the reader should consist in the literary absurdity and microcosmic rough-and-tumble fun of the action, which suggests some Hellenistic Mickey Mouse cartoon.

1972

THE HOMERIC HYMNS

I. TO DIONYSUS

Some say it was at Dracanum, and some on the island of Naxos,   1
Others on windswept Icarus, heavenly infant Twice Born;
Others maintain by the deep-swirling stream of the Alpheus river
Semele bore you, begotten by Zeus, whose delight is in thunder;
Others, O Lord, say at Thebes you were born: they are all of them liars.   5
Zeus it was, father of gods and of men, who gave birth to you far from
Mankind, concealing the fact of your birth from his wife, white-armed
     Hera.
There is a certain high mountain called Nysa, which flowers with forests,
Far far away in Phoenicia, not far from the rivers of Egypt . . .

And many decorative images shall they establish in temples.   10
As he divided in three, so every third year in your honor,
Making immaculate hecatombs, men will perform sacrifices.
So with his coal-colored eyebrows assented the scion of Cronus,
And the ambrosial locks of the monarch were shaken about him,
Back from his immortal brow; and he caused great Olympus to tremble.   15
Thus, when he spoke, did the counselor, Zeus, with his head give
     commandment.

Twice-born distracter of women, be kind! It is you that the poets
Sing to begin with and when they conclude. There is not any way by
Which to recall sacred song if a person should ever forget you.
Farewell, twice-born Dionysus! Yourself and your reverend mother,   20
Semele, Cadmus's daughter, whom some people know as Thyone.

II. TO DEMETER

1   Awesome Demeter, the goddess with beautiful hair, I begin to
    Sing about, her and her trim-ankled daughter, whom Aidoneus[1]
    Raped or was given by Zeus, the deep thunderer widely discerning,
    When she was playing apart from her mother, Demeter, the golden
5   Giver of glorious fruit, with the deep-bosomed daughters of Ocean,
    Gathering flowers, the roses and crocus that grow in the midst of
    Deep, grassy meadows as well as fair lilies and hyacinths, iris,
    And the narcissus, which earth at the bidding of Zeus had produced to
    Please the Receiver of Many, a snare for the flower-faced maiden,
10 Glistening miracle, marvel and wonder to all who behold it,
    Whether the gods, who are deathless, or men, who are born but to
        perish.
    For from its root it thrust upward a glorious, manifold blossom,
    And it exuded a fragrance so sweet that broad heaven above and
    All the earth laughed with pleasure, as did the salt wave of the sea. The
15 Maiden was struck with amazement and reached out with both of her
        hands to
    Seize the desirable plaything. Then earth, the extensively traveled,
    Gaped in the prairie of Nysa, and He Who Has Several Names, the
    Monarch Who Welcomes So Many, the underworld offspring of Cronus
    Leapt, with his immortal horses, straight out of the chasm upon her,
20 Catching her up on his glittering chariot—she was unwilling—
    Carried her off still complaining; she wailed at the top of her voice and

1. Hades.

Called on her father, the Highest and Best, the successor of Cronus.
Nobody heard her, however, not one of the undying gods, nor
Men, who are born but to perish, not even the rich-fruited olives,
No one but Persaeus's daughter, considerate Hecate, heard her,   25
Wearing a radiant headdress at home in the depth of her cave, and
Helios's lordship, Hyperion's glorious son: they both heard the
Maiden invoking her father, the scion of Cronus, who sat far
Off and apart from the gods in his worshipful temple, receiving
Manifold human petitions and beautiful offerings from humans.   30
It was with Zeus's connivance that Hades, his paternal brother,
Host and Director of Many, the Lord Who Has Several Titles,
Cronus's notorious son, had abducted the maid all reluctant,
Driving his immortal horses. So long as the goddess beheld the
Earth and the stars in the sky and the beams of the sun and the roaring   35
Sea full of fish, and the maiden expected the sight of her noble
Mother as well as her kindred, the gods, who are ever-begotten,
Hope still enchanted her generous spirit in spite of her anguish.

Then did the heights of the mountains, and then did the depths of the
    ocean
Echo her immortal voice; she was heard by her reverend mother.   40
Keen was the anguish that seized on her heart, so she tore off the
    headdress
From her ambrosial hair, and she rent it with both of her dear hands;
Shedding the coal-colored cloak from her shoulders, she fled like a
    seabird
Over the wet and the dry ways of earth in pursuit of her daughter.
No one was willing to tell her what happened exactly and fully,   45
Neither her undying kindred nor men, who are born but to perish;
None of the birds, as reliable messenger, flew to Demeter.
Searching, the Reverend Mother then wandered on earth, holding
    kindled
Torches aloft in her hands for nine days and nine nights without tasting

50 Either ambrosia or the sweet beverage nectar, in mourning,
Not even bathing her body. But when the tenth radiant morning
Shone upon earth, she encountered dear Hecate, carrying brightness
Held in her hands, who addressed her by name as if bringing her
tidings,
"Holy Demeter, great bringer of seasons and glorious giver,
55 Which of the heavenly gods or of men, who are born but to perish,
Has, by abducting Persephone, thus so afflicted your dear heart?
I heard her voice, but I did not behold who it was with my own eyes.
Briefly have I told you everything that I can honestly tell you."
Thus she concluded. And never a word did the daughter of Rhea
60 Answer, but swiftly she darted away with her, holding the blazing
Torches on high, till they came to the sun, overseer of gods and
Men; and then, standing in front of his horses, the goddess addressed
him.
"Helios, now, if I ever have gladdened your heart or your humor
Once, by a deed or a word perhaps, pity me, though I'm a goddess.
65 Her whom I bore, the superlative flower of beauty, the Maiden,
Hers was the voice that I heard as it thrilled through the harvestless
aether,
As if she were being forced; but I did not observe it at firsthand.
You upon every land and on every body of water
Out of the glittering atmosphere blaze down your radiant sunbeams.
70 Tell me exactly about my dear child, if you happened to see her.
Who was it seized her and took her against her will forcibly from me?
One of the undying gods or a man who was born but to perish?"
That was her question. The son of Hyperion answered her briefly.
"Madame Demeter, almighty and beautiful daughter of Rhea,
75 You shall be told, for I greatly revere you and pity your grieving
Over your trim-ankled daughter. Now nobody else is to blame, no
God but cloud-carrying Zeus, for he gave her to Hades, his brother,
For his intended, to call her his blossoming bride; as for Hades,
Snatching her up on his horses, he bore her off loudly lamenting

Under the earth to his kingdom of murk and perennial darkness.   80
Nevertheless, mighty goddess, desist from extravagant mourning;
It is not proper in vain to indulge your insatiate anger.
Aidoneus, the Ruler of Many, is not an unlikely
Son-in-law; he is your brother. And furthermore, he obtained worship
At the first triple division of worlds, when their doom was decided,   85
Dwelling with those over whom Hades' lot once appointed him ruler."
Helios, when he had spoken the foregoing, called to his horses,
And they, obedient, drew the swift chariot rapidly, birdlike.
Anguish more bitter and violent entered the heart of Demeter.
Angry, henceforth, with the black-clouded king of the gods, she avoided   90
Heavenly meetings and lofty Olympus. She went in disguise from
City to city of men and the splendid achievements of mankind,
Wasting her looks a great while, so that nobody, whether of men or
Broad-girdled women, would recognize her upon sight, till she reached
   the
Home of sharp-witted Celeus, the ruler of fragrant Eleusis.[2]   95
Deo[3] sat down at the roadside, consuming her dear heart with sorrow
Next to the Spring of the Maiden, where women who lived in the city
Came for their water, in shade, for above it there flourished an olive.
Like an old woman she was in appearance, one born in the distant
Past who has long outworn childbed and has no more part in the gifts of   100
Her Who Loves Wreaths, Aphrodite—of such are the nurses of children
Or, in the echoing mansions of kings who administer justice,
Housekeepers; such she appeared to the four Eleusinian maidens
Coming to fetch the available water back home in their brazen
Pitchers unto the affectionate home of their father, Celeus—   105
Four of them, lovely as goddesses, still in the flower of girlhood,
Namely, Callidice, Demo, and pretty Cleisidice, with their

    2. In Eleusis, north of Athens, were celebrated the holiest mysteries of the ancient
world, those of Demeter and Persephone; their initiates were sworn to a secrecy so pro-
found that we know little about them.
    3. Another name for Demeter.

Older sister, Callithoe. None of them recognized Deo:
Difficult are the immortals for mortals to know when they see them.
110 Standing nearby, they addressed her in words that flew straight to their
    target.
  "Who are you? Where are you coming from, grandmother, one of the
    old folk?
  Why have you strayed from the city? Why don't you draw near to the
    houses?
  There, women your age and younger there are in the shadowy great
    halls,
  Ready to show you affection not only in words but in action."
115 Thus they expressed themselves; reverend Deo replied to them, saying,
  "Daughters, whoever you are, for I see that indeed you are women,
  Greetings! I willingly tell you my story; it isn't improper
  That I should tell you the truth, since you earnestly ask me to do so.
  Doso my name is, my reverend mother imposed it upon me.
120 Recently, over the breadth of the sea I unwillingly crossed from
  Crete—yes, unwillingly: pirates abducted me forcibly, using
  Strength of necessity. In their swift vessel they landed, soon after,
  Somewhere near Thoricus. There, all the women in bands went ashore,
    the
  Menfolk accompanied them. In the shade of the prow of their ship, they
125 Spread out their supper. My heart was not set on the tasty repast, so
  Secretly slipping away in the darkness cross-country, I quickly
  Fled from my arrogant masters in order they might not enjoy my
  Ransom who'd carried me off so, like booty unbought, or unpaid for!
  Wandering, I have come here, and I do not have any idea
130 What is the name of this country or who its inhabitants may be.
  But I pray those who inhabit Olympian mansions to give you
  Suitable husbands and birth of such children as mothers desire.
  Pardon me, maidens, which man's or what woman's abode, my dear
    children,
  Would I be wise to approach in my search for employment befitting

One who is no longer young? Woman's work I will gladly perform, and   135
Holding a newly born baby secure in my arms, I should nurse him
Beautifully; I can do housework and make master's bed in the alcove
Of the well-carpentered bedroom, and see to the work of the women."
Thus spoke the goddess, and straightway replied the inviolate maiden,
Pretty Callidice, best in appearance of Celeus's daughters: 140
"Mother, the gifts of the gods humankind must endure, though
   afflicted.
They are much stronger than we are. And now I shall clearly instruct
   you,
Naming the men hereabouts who possess greatest influence for their
Respectability, those who stand out in the populace, who keep
By their advice and their upright decisions our citadel scatheless.   145
Prudent Triptolemus, honest Diocles, and good Polyxenus,
Blameless Eumolpus, and Dolichus, and our respectable father—
All of them eminent persons, with wives to look after their households.
And, of the women, not one on first sight would dismiss you offhand or
Send you away from her door disrespectfully, slighting your aspect;   150
Rather will they all receive you because you appear like a goddess.
Now, if you like to abide here, then we will go back to our father's
House and relate to our mother, the handsomely dressed Metaneira,
All from beginning to end that has happened, so she will invite you
Home to our house, and you need not go making such inquiries   155
   elsewhere.
Our little brother, her last-born and darling, is nursed in the palace,
Subject of much supplication and heartily welcomed at last there.
If you should bring the boy up till he came to the measure of manhood,
Anyone seeing you soon—any woman—would envy you for the
Gifts which I know that our mother would give in reward for his   160
   raising."
Such was the speech of the maiden; the goddess agreed with a nod.
   Then,
Filling their glistening vessels with water, they carried them proudly;

Soon they had come to the house of their father, and quickly related
What they had seen to their mother and what they had heard, and at
    once she
165 Bade them go summon the stranger, whatever she asked for in wages.
Then, like young hinds, or like heifers that gambol in Spring in the
    meadows
Once they have fed to their hearts' satisfaction, they picked up the edges
Of their impeccable shifts, and they darted along down the hollow
Chariot path, with their crocuslike hair floating over their shoulders.
170 Soon they discovered the reverend goddess at rest where they left her,
Right by the roadside, and then they conducted her to their beloved
Father's abode, and she followed behind them, consuming her dear
    heart,
Grief stricken; veiled was her head, and about the dear goddess's narrow
Feet the deep fringe of her sea-colored overcloak rustled like water.
175 Soon they approached the affectionate home of their god-nurtured
    father.
Entering through the verandah, they came on their ladylike mother
Seated, her back to a pillar that held up the tightly made ceiling,
Holding her newly born babe to her breast, her new darling. Her
    daughters
Ran to their mother. The goddess, however, in crossing the threshold,
180 Reached to the roof with her head, filled the doorway with heavenly
    splendor.
Reverence, awe, and a sickening terror possessed Metaneira,
So she arose from her chair and invited her guest to be seated.
Deo, the bringer of seasons and giver of glorious gifts, not
Wishing to sit on the glittering chair, without speaking a long while,
185 Stood with her beautiful eyes on the ground, till good-hearted Iambe
Brought her a carpentered stool, after throwing a silvery sheepskin
Over it. There sat the goddess, upholding her veil in her hands in
Front of her face, without utterance, grief stricken, mute on the
    footstool

For a long while, neither greeting by gesture or word anybody,
Silent, unsmiling, refusing to taste either liquid or solid,   190
Wasting away in incessant desire for her trim-ankled daughter,
Until kind-hearted Iambe, by means of her many facetious
Sayings and mockery, roused the most holy and reverend goddess
First to a smile, then to laughter and something resembling good
    humor.
Often at seasons thereafter, she flattered the goddess's bad moods.   195
Then Metaneira presented a cup full of sweet-tasting wine, which
Deo refused, for she said that she was not permitted to taste red
Wine, but she asked them to give her instead a concoction of barley
Water to drink, in a beverage flavored with delicate mint leaves.
So they concocted the potion the goddess requested, and brought it.   200
Deo accepted this drink for the sake of the sacrament, gravely.
Handsomely girt Metaneira began to attempt conversation.
"Greetings, good woman. I do not suppose you descended from
    baseborn
Parents, but rather from noble, for dignity shines in your eyes, and
Grace, as they shine from the faces of kings who administer justice.   205
Ah, humankind must endure all the gifts of the gods, though we suffer
Out of necessity, seeing their yoke has been laid on our shoulders.
Now that you've come here, whatever is mine will be yours to dispose
    of.
Take, then, this child unto nurse—my dear son, lately born and
    unlooked-for,
Whom the immortals have sent me in answer to my supplication.   210
If you will bring up the boy till he comes to the measure of manhood,
Anyone seeing you then, any woman, will envy you, for the
Gifts that I promise his mother will give in reward for his raising."
Thus did Demeter, a goddess once gorgeously garlanded, answer:
"Greetings, good woman, as well, in return: may the gods give you good   215
    things!
As for your son, I will gladly accept him to nurse, as you ask me;

Yes, and I hope through no fault of his nurse will enchantment afflict
    him.
I know a powerful antidote for the discomfort of toothache,
I know an excellent bulwark against the most mischievous magic."
220 When she had said this, she gathered him into her sweet-smelling
    bosom
With her ambrosial hands, and the heart of his mother was gladdened.
Thus it befell that Demeter brought up in the palace the brilliant
Demophoon, son of sharp-witted Celeus and fair Metaneira.
Quickly he grew and waxed strong, like a true supernatural being,
225 Eating no food, neither fed at the breast of his mother. Demeter
Rubbed him instead with ambrosia, like one engendered of heaven,
Fragrantly breathing upon him and holding the child in her bosom.
Nightly she buried him deep in the midst of the fire, like a firebrand,
All unbeknownst to his parents, to whom it appeared a great wonder
230 How he was growing precocious and how he resembled the gods. And
She might have made him immortal and ageless, except for the folly
Of well-girt Metaneira who, spying one night from her chamber,
Saw what the goddess was doing. She shrieked and belabored her flanks
    in
Terror, hysterical over her son and distracted in mind, and
235 As she lamented, she uttered the following hasty expressions:
"Demophoon, darling! Behold where the outlandish woman has hid
    you
Right in the midst of the fire, to my grief and unbearable anguish!"
So she exclaimed in her grievance; the queen among goddesses heard
    her.
Furious therefore, once gorgeously garlanded Lady Demeter
240 Snatched from the fire with her immortal hands the dear child
    Metaneira
Bore in the palace unhoped-for, and brusquely rejected the infant
From her immortal embrace to the ground, being dreadfully angry.
At the same time, she admonished exquisitely girt Metaneira:

"Witless are humans and gross, inconsiderate, thoughtless, and stupid!
Lacking foreknowledge of fate, whether evil or good will befall them.   245
You in your folly have erred to the highest degree, Metaneira.
Witness the pitiless waters of Styx, the great oath of the gods, that
I should have made your dear son an immortal and furthermore ageless
All of his days, and moreover had given him evergreen honor.
Now he has not any way of escaping from death and misfortune.   250
Nevertheless, an unwithered renown will attach to him always,
Since he has lain on my lap and has slept in the arms of a goddess.
But, with the full revolution of years and succession of seasons,
He shall experience strife: Eleusinians, sons of their fathers,
Waging incessantly war internecine, with battle- and war-cry.   255
I am Demeter the Venerable, to immortals and mortals
Mightiest source of delight and of physical sustenance also.
Go now and build me a sizable temple, an altar beneath it;
Let the whole populace build it, in sight of the citadel's steep walls,
Over the Spring Callichorus, upon a conspicuous hillside.[4]   260
I shall instruct you myself in my mysteries, so that hereafter,
When you perform them, you may do so piously, winning my favor."
When she had spoken, the goddess transfigured her size and
　　appearance,
Shedding old age. Circumambient beauty was wafted about her;
From her odiferous garments diffused a delectable perfume;   265
From her immortal, ambrosial body a radiance shone; her
Corn-colored hair tumbled over her shoulders; the comfortable house
　　was
Filled with a brightness of lightning. Demeter went out through the
　　palace.
Poor Metaneira! Her knees were immediately loosened, a long while
She remained speechless, completely forgetting to pick up her darling   270

4. A walled citadel required an internal source of water and a situation of advantage.
Callichorus ("fairly dancing") was the spring for Eleusis, the site of the great religious
mysteries in honor of Demeter and Persephone.

Child from the ground. But his sisters, on hearing his piteous outcry,
Leapt from their comfortable beds, and while one took him up in her
    arms and
Cradled the child in her bosom, another rekindled the fire,
While yet another was running on tiptoe to waken their mother.
275 Then they all gathered about him and, washing the struggling infant,
Cuddled and kissed him, in vain, for his heart was not comforted
    thereby,
Feeling inferior nurses and worse foster mothers now held him.
Nightlong, while quaking with dread, they placated the reverend
    goddess,
And at the dawn's first appearance, they told the whole story to widely
280 Ruling Celeus, exactly as beautiful Deo commanded.
Summoning to an assembly his numerous people, he bade them
Make for the richly coiffed goddess an opulent temple and altar
On the conspicuous hillside. And they very quickly obeyed him,
Hearkening to his instruction, and built it as he had enjoined them.
285 As for the infant, he flourished like some supernatural being.
When they'd completed the building and rested a while from their
    labor,
Severally they went home. But Demeter, whose hair is like ripe corn,
Sitting apart from the blessed immortals, from all of her kindred,
Waited and wasted away with regret for her trim-ankled daughter.
290 Then a most terrible year over all the inhabited earth she
Caused for mankind, and a cruel. The soil did not let any seedlings
Come to the surface: Demeter, once handsomely garlanded, hid them.
Many a crescent-shaped plowshare the oxen in vain dragged through
    furrows;
Much was the colorless barley that fell without fruit on the good earth.
295 Now were the race of articulate men altogether destroyed by
Hardship and famine, depriving the gods who inhabit Olympus
Of their invidious worship, their honors and sacrifice, had not
Zeus taken thought and considered what ought to be done to prevent it.

First, he dispatched golden Iris to fly to and summon his sister,
Fair-haired Demeter, whose form is admired and desired of so many.   300
Thus her commission, and Iris obeyed the black-clouded son of
Cronus, and rapidly ran on swift feet through the space intervening
Till she arrived at a citadel fragrant with incense, Eleusis,
Where, in her temple, she found the deep-blue-mantled goddess
        Demeter,
Whom she addressed in this wise, using words that flew straight to their   305
        target.
"All-father Zeus, he whose thoughts are unwithered and deathless,
        Demeter,
Calls you to come to your kind and the gods who're engendered forever.
Go, then, and let not my message from heaven remain
        unaccomplished!"
Iris besought her; the heart of the earth-mother was not persuaded.
Then father Zeus must dispatch all the blessed and ever-abiding   310
Gods, till, one after another, they came and they called upon Deo,
Giving her manifold beautiful gifts and the deference due her,
Which she desired to receive at the hands of the other immortals.
No one, however, was able to sway her emotions or conscious
Mind. She was angry at heart, and she sternly rejected their speeches,   315
Saying she never again would set foot upon fragrant Olympus,
Never would suffer the corn and the fruit of the earth to awaken
Till she beheld with her own eyes the face of her lovely daughter.
When father Zeus, the widely discerning deep thunderer, heard this,
He into Erebus sent the destroyer of Argus with his gold   320
Wand, so that when with soft words he had talked over obdurate Hades,
He might lead holy Persephone out of the visible darkness
Into the light and the company of the immortals, so then her
Mother, Demeter, beholding her child, might abate her resentment.
Hermes was not disobedient. Quitting the throne of Olympus,   325
He with alacrity leapt and descended to underground chasms,
Where he discovered the Ruler at home in the midst of his palace,

Seated upon a divan at the side of his worshipful consort.
Very unwilling she was, on account of her longing for mother,
330 Who afar off, all because of the deeds of the blessed immortals,
Brooded upon her design. Then the powerful slayer of Argus,
Standing in decent proximity, spoke to the Ruler as follows.
"Hades with coal-colored ringlets, dictator of those that have perished,
All-father Zeus has commanded me forthwith to fetch back the Maiden,
335 Noble Persephone, out of the underworld so that her mother
May, at the sight of her daughter, desist from her anger and dreadful
Fury against the immortals. For know that she meditates mighty
Deeds: the destruction of feeble mankind from the face of the earth by
Hiding the seeds underground and thus utterly blasting the worship
340 Of the immortals. She harbors a dreadful resentment, no longer
Visits the gods, but she sits in her incense-odiferous temple
Far away, holding the rocky acropolis over Eleusis."
When he had finished, the Lord of the Underworld, Aidoneus,
Lifted his eyebrows and smiled. Nonetheless he obeyed the behest of
345 Zeus, for he summoned and said to sharp-witted Persephone quickly,
"Go, then, Persephone, back to the arms of your sable-robed mother,
Keeping a gentle and kind disposition and heart in your bosom.
Do not indulge in excessive despondency more than is proper.
I shall, among the immortals, not prove an unsuitable husband,
350 Being your father's own brother, the brother of Zeus. In this kingdom
You shall be mistress of everything living and creeping and have the
Greatest proportion of honor among the immortals. Eternal
Shall be the penalties of those transgressors hereafter whoever
Fail to propitiate your mighty godhead by sacrifice and the
355 Pious performance of rites and the payment of suitable presents."
When he had spoken, exceedingly clever Persephone was glad;
Blithely she leapt up, delighted. But Hades himself gave her something
Edible covertly, namely, a sweet pomegranate seed, just one,
Peering about him suspiciously, so that she should not abide the
360 Rest of her days at the side of her mother, impressive Demeter.

Hades, the Ruler of Many, then harnessed his immortal horses
Unto the front of his glittering chariot, which she ascended.
Standing beside her then, Hermes, the powerful slayer of Argus,
Taking the whip and the reins between both of his capable dear hands,
Drove through the hall of the dead, and the horses were nothing   365
    unwilling.
Flying, they quickly traversed the long journey before them, and neither
Seas nor the water of rivers nor green grassy glens in the mountains
Nor mountain peaks ever checked the career of the immortal horses—
Over all these lay their course as they cleft through the fathomless
    aether.
Hermes, their driver, drew up right in front of the sweet-smelling   370
    temple
Where the once beautifully garlanded goddess Demeter was waiting.
When she got sight of her daughter, she dashed like a madwoman down
    the
Forested side of the mountain. Persephone, seeing the beaming
Eyes of her mother, abandoned both horses and driver, and leaping
Down from the chariot, ran to her, fell on her neck, and embraced her.   375
Even as Deo was holding Persephone safe in her arms, her
Mind had begun to suspect some deception. She anxiously trembled,
Checked her affectionate greeting a moment, and asked her a question.
"Darling, while you were there, underground, tell me, you did not
    partake, or
Did you? of any refreshment? Speak out. Do not try to conceal it.   380
Better that both of us know. If you didn't, now you have arisen,
Dear, from the side of detestable Hades, with me and your father,
Cronus's umbrageous successor, and honored by all the immortals
Shall you abide. If you did, you must, fluttering back underneath the
Chasms of earth, make your dwelling a third of the year and its seasons 385
There, and the other two seasons with me and the other immortals.
But when the earth is abloom with the various flowers of springtime,
Then from the palpable darkness again you shall rise, a great wonder

Both to the undying gods and to men who are born but to perish.
390 Now, tell me just by what ruse the Receiver of Many deceived you."
Then very lovely Persephone said to her mother in answer,
"Mother, to you I will tell the whole story exactly and frankly.
When the swift messenger Hermes, the luck bringer, came to me saying,
At the command of my father—of Zeus—and the other immortals,
395 That I should come out of Erebus so at my sight you might cease from
Anger against the immortals, abating your terrible fury,
Blithely I leapt for delight, but my Lord surreptitiously gave me
One pomegranate seed—one—a delicious and delicate morsel
Which he compelled me by force and against my desire to swallow.
400 Now, how he first caught me up, by the closely laid plan of my father,
Zeus, and then carried me off into vast subterranean chasms,
I shall explain, as you ask me, and tell from beginning to end. As
All of us girls were disporting ourselves in a lovely meadow—
Leucippe, Phaeno, Electra, Ianthe, Iache, Melite,
405 Rhode and sweet Callirhoe as well, Melobosis and Tyche,
Rhodope, darling Calypso, Urania, Styx, Galaxaura,
Pallas, who rouses to battle, and Artemis, strewer of arrows:
All of us playing, and plucking by handfuls adorable blossoms,
Delicate crocuses mingled with iris and hyacinth, cup-shaped
410 Roses and lilies together, a wonderful sight to behold, and
Also the fatal narcissus that broad earth produced like a crocus.
This I was plucking for joy when the earth underneath me gaped vastly;
Out leapt that powerful lord, the Receiver of Many, and bore me
Under the earth on his gold-plated chariot. Very unwilling
415 Was I, I shouted aloud at the top of my voice, but in vain. And
There, though it causes me many a pang, I have told you the whole
  truth."
Mother and daughter the whole of the day in unanimous humor
Thereupon gladdened each other in heart and in mind very greatly,
Clinging together in love till their spirits abated their sorrows.
420 Mutual pleasures and joys they received and they gave one another.

Hecate, she of the glittering headdress, came into their presence,
Frequently kissed with affection the daughter of holy Demeter.
Henceforth, that lady became to Persephone servant and handmaid.
Golden-haired Rhea, his mother, deep-thundering, widely discerning
Zeus had appointed as envoy to summon the sable-cloaked goddess   425
Back to her kindred, the gods, where he promised to give her such honors
And she desired to obtain in the company of the immortals.
Thus, he decreed that her daughter should dwell a third part of the
    turning
Year under vaporous darkness, the other two parts with her mother
And with the other immortals; and Rhea obeyed his commission.   430
Down from the heights of Olympus she darted, imperious, till she
Came to the Rharian plain, a rich, life-giving udder of plowland
Once, but now not at all life-giving: fallow it stood and all leafless.
By the design of fair-ankled Demeter, the barley lay hidden.
Not long thereafter, the plain would be coiffed with the corn's narrow   435
    ears when
Spring turned to summer, and while the rich furrows were laden with
    corn stalks,
Others were bound into sheaves. Such the spot where the goddess first
    landed
From the unharvested air. When they gladly beheld one another,
Both of the goddesses' hearts were rejoiced. And then brightly crowned
    Rhea
Said to her, "Come here, my child, deep-thundering, widely   440
    discerning
Zeus summons you to your kindred, the gods, and he promises you such
Honors as you may desire in the company of the immortals.
And he decrees that the Maiden shall dwell a third part of the turning
Year under vaporous darkness, the other two parts with her mother
And with the other immortals. And thus his pronouncement, 'So be it!'   445
Sealed with a nod of his head. Therefore, come, my dear child, and obey
    him,

Be not incessantly wroth with the black-clouded scion of Cronus!
Soon make the life-giving fruits of the earth again flourish for
    mankind."
Rhea had spoken; Demeter, fair-garlanded, was not unwilling.

450 Soon from the clod-cluttered furrows, she made the rich harvest of
    grain spring,
So the whole breadth of the earth was encumbered with leaves and with
    flowers.
Paying a visit, in turn, to the kings who administer justice—
Noble Triptolemus, princely Diocles, the drover of horses,
Mighty Eumolpus, Celeus, the leader of people—Demeter

455 Showed them her ritual service and taught them her mysteries, even
Diocles, princely Triptolemus, and Polyxenus, the solemn
Mysteries, which are unthinkable either to question or utter
Or to transgress: for a holy respect checks the utterance of them.
Happy the man who, of those that inhabit this earth, has beheld them!

460 The uninitiate, one without part in the ritual, never
Gets any portion of similar benefits, blessings, whatever,
Once he has perished and passed away under the vaporous darkness.
After the queen among goddesses had inculcated these matters,
She and her daughter returned to Olympus' divine congregation,

465 Where they have ever a dwelling with Zeus, who delights in the thunder:
Solemn and reverend goddesses! Happy indeed is the man whom
These ladies love, of all people who dwell on the earth, with
    aforethought.
Soon they will send to his fireside Plutus, the giver of riches,
Wealth and abundance and plenty to men, who are born but to perish.

470 Goddesses holding in fee the republic of fragrant Eleusis,
Paros amid the encircling waters, and stony Antrona,
Mistress and bringer of seasons, queen, glorious giver, Demeter,
You and your excellent, beautiful daughter, Persephone, Maiden,
Kindly in thanks for this poem assure me a pleasant subsistence,

475 And I shall try to remember another about you and sing it!

III. TO APOLLO

To Delian Apollo

I shall remember and never pass over the marksman Apollo,   1
Whom, as he goes through the palace of Zeus, the gods tremble in front
    of,
All of them rising in haste from their seats when Apollo approaches,
Bending his luminous bow: that is, all of the gods except Leto,
Leto alone who sits still at His side Whose delight is in thunder,   5
Zeus. She relaxes the bow of Apollo and fastens his quiver,
Taking his archery in her own hands from his powerful shoulders.
Hanging it on a gold peg on a pillar beside which his father
Sits, she conducts her great son to a chair of his own where she seats
    him.
His father Zeus then presents him a goblet of gold filled with nectar,   10
Welcoming home his dear son, whereupon all the other immortals
Sit themselves down in their places. Now ladylike Leto rejoices
Since she gave birth to a bowman, a son of some physical prowess.
Leto, rejoice! You are blessed, for you have borne glorious children,
Namely, Apollo, the Master, and Artemis, Strewer of Arrows,   15
Her on the isle of Ortygia, him on precipitous Delos,
Where you supported yourself as you lay on the hillside of Cynthus,
Your back to the broad mountainside, by a palm, near the brook of
    Inopus.

How should I hymn you, Apollo, so handsomely sung of already?
Yours is the principle, Phoebus, of verse universally laid down   20

Both on the continent, breeder of heifers, and over the islands,
All of whose lookouts and headlands are pleasing to you, as are lofty
Peaks of the mountains, as well as the rivers that flow to the salt sea,
Beaches that slope to the water and Mediterranean havens.

25 Say, shall I tell how first Leto gave birth to you, joy of all mankind,
Leaning against Cynthus's mountainside on the precipitous isle of
Delos, surrounded by treacherous currents: from alternate sides a
Dark wave was driving to land under winds that were whistling shrilly.
Thence was your origin; now you are lord over all that is mortal:

30 Those that the island of Crete holds within it, the city of Athens,
Also the island of Aegina, famous for dockyards Euboea,
Aegae as well as Eiresia, close to the sea Peparethos,
Thracian Athos, and Pelion's towering pinnacles also,
Thracian Samos as well as the shadowy mountains of Ida,

35 Scyros, Phocaea—"Seal Island"—precipitous, steep Autocane,
Civilized Imbros on one hand, and then inhospitable Lemnos,
Heavenly Lesbos, the dwelling of Makar, the son of Aeolus,
Chios, which of all the islands that lie in the sea is the brightest,
Asperous Mimas, all crags, and the cliffs of the cape of Corycus,

40 Brilliantly glistening Claros, the mountain of steep Aesagea,
Samos, abounding in streams, the vertiginous heights of Mycale,
Lovely Miletus, and Cos, prehistoric Meropian city,
Cnidus, which rises abrupt from the sea, lonely, windswept Carpathus,
Not only Naxos but Paros, as well as petrific Rhenaea:

45 Such were the lands Leto visited when in travail with Apollo,
Asking if any of them would be willing to welcome her offspring.
Gravely they trembled and quaked and were very afraid, all these places;
None of them, however prosperous, dared to receive the god Phoebus,
Until majestical Leto set foot on the island of Delos,

50 To which she shortly addressed winged words in the form of a question.
"Delos, do you want to be the elected abode of my offspring
Phoebus Apollo—and to him establish an opulent temple?
Nobody else, it is obvious, ever is likely to touch you.

I do not think you are going to do well with herds or with flocks, nor
Shall you bear vineyards; indeed, you will never grow much, that is   55
    certain.
But if the temple were yours, of Apollo, the accurate marksman,
Men of all nations would gather here, bringing their hecatombs with
    them,
So that unspeakable odor of sacrifice always will hover
Over your country, and you shall provide and sustain those who hold you
Out of the hand of the stranger, because your own soil is infertile."   60
So she declared, and the island was glad and in answer addressed her,
"Leto, most honored of goddesses, daughter of mighty Coeus,
Willingly would I make welcome the birth of his far-darting Lordship,
For, it is horribly true, I have evil repute among mankind,
And by this means, after all, I might come to be highly respected.   65
But at a word do I tremble, and, Leto, I shall not conceal it.
This is the reason: they say that Apollo will be very haughty
And overbearing, a somebody, president of the immortals
As of the mortals that perish on earth with its wheat-growing farmland.
Thus do I dreadfully fear in my heart and my sensitive feelings,   70
Lest, on that day when your glorious offspring shall first see the
    sunlight,
He shall despise me, an island, because my poor soil is so rocky,
And, with his feet overturning me, spurn me beneath the salt billow,
Where the great waves will wash over my head in abundance forever.
Then he will just go away to some other land that may attract him,   75
There to construct his great temple and grove and luxurious arbor.
In me the polyp and octopus will build their chambers, the black seals
May make their homes in me free from anxiety, since I lack people.
But if you would undertake, mighty goddess, to swear a great oath that
Here he will build his original, gorgeously beautiful temple   80
To be a famous oracular shrine for mankind, then thereafter
Let him construct all the temples and precincts and groves that he
    pleases

For all the rest of mankind! Surely, he will have plenty of titles!"
So said the island, and Leto pronounced the great oath of the gods:
   "Now
85 Earth bear me witness in this, and the heavens extending above us,
Also the trickling water of Styx, which is reckoned the greatest
And the most terrible oath that exists, by the blessed immortals:
Sure shall the incense-odiferous altar of Phoebus stand ever
Here, and his precinct, and you will have honor surpassing all others."
90 When she had sworn the great oath of the gods and completed her
    promise,
Delos sincerely rejoiced at the birth of the far-darting master.
Leto, however, was pierced for nine days and nine nights by unwonted
Pains in her labor. The goddesses, all of them, came to assist her,
Those of the highest importance, Dione, for instance, and Rhea,
95 Themis, detector of crime, and the voice of the sea, Amphitrite,
Others divine and immortal as well, all but Hera, the white armed,
Who was enthroned in the palace of Zeus, the controller of storm
    clouds.
But Eileithyia, the goddess of childbirth, heard nothing about it,
Seated on top of Olympus, because of the cunning of Hera,
100 Under the luminous cover of gold-tinted clouds, where the white-
    armed
Goddess detained her because of her jealous hostility unto
Lovely-haired Leto, about to give birth to a handsome and strong son.
Presently, Leto's supporters dispatched from the livable island
Iris to fetch Eileithyia, her wage a magnificent necklace
105 Nine cubits long, which they promised her, strung upon solid gold
    wires.
And they instructed her how to approach her in secret apart from
Hera, lest she by her speeches divert her thereafter from going.
Swift as the wind, nifty Iris, when she had heard all their instructions
Started to run, and she quickly completed the distance between and
110 Came to the seat of the gods, the vertiginous height of Olympus.

When she had called Eileithyia to step from the hall to the doorway
Instantly, Iris addressed her in words that went straight to their target,
Telling her all that the goddesses bade her that dwelt on Olympus,
Till she completely persuaded her heart and affectionate feelings.
Then they departed together, like timorous doves in their movements.   115
When Eileithyia, the goddess of childbirth, set foot upon Delos,
Labor seized hold upon Leto. She painfully wanted to give birth
Then, so, embracing a palm tree, she knelt in the green grassy meadow,
Bracing herself on her knees. And the earth smiled with pleasure
    beneath her.
Out then he leapt to the light, and the goddesses shouted together,   120
"Aie!" and, Phoebus, they took you and washed you in beautiful water,
Clean and according to ritual, wrapping a delicate white cloth,
Recently woven, about you, and fastened it round with a gold cord.
Nor did his mother give suck to Apollo, who carried the gold sword.
Themis, however, with her own immortal hands, offered him nectar,   125
Also delightful ambrosia. Leto, moreover, was happy,
Since she had borne a great bowman, a son of some physical prowess.
But when you merely had tasted, O Phoebus, that heavenly diet,
Neither the cords made of gold could contain you for all of your
    struggles,
Nor could your wrappings restrain you, the ends of them all being   130
    loosened.
Straightway, then, Phoebus Apollo conversed with the goddesses,
    saying,
"So—let the lyre be dear to me, equally dear be the curved bow!
And I shall prophesy Zeus's infallible meaning to mankind."
When he had spoken these words, he set foot upon earth's broad
    foundation,
Phoebus, the long haired, the long-distance archer, and all the immortal   135
Goddesses marveled. The island of Delos all over was fraught with
Gold at the sight of the offspring of Zeus and of Leto, because of
Flattered delight that Apollo had chosen it over the other

Islands and over the mainland, on which to establish his home and
140 Loved it beyond all the others at heart, so the island of Delos
Blossomed, as sometimes the ridge of a mountain, with flowers of the
    forest.
As for yourself, mighty master and silver-bowed marksman, Apollo,
Typically, now you set foot on the difficult slopes of Mount Cynthus,
Now you meandered from island to island to various peoples.
145 Many magnificent temples and leafy luxurious bowers,
Headlands and lookouts are dear to you, also the prominent, pointed
Peaks of the mountains as well as the rivers that flow to the ocean.
Yet most of all you indulge your affection in Delos, O Phoebus,
Where the Ionians gather in honor of you, with their trailing
150 Tunics—themselves and their children and modest and reverent
    spouses—
As in remembrance of you they take pleasure in boxing and dancing,
Also in song on occasion, whenever they hold their assembly.
If he were present when all the Ionians gathered together,
One would declare that they must be immortal and ageless forever
155 When he beheld the great physical grace of them all, and his heart was
Glad at the sight of the men, and women so handsomely girdled,
With the swift ships that belong to them also, and all their possessions.
And, what is more, a great marvel, the fame of which never shall perish:
Maidens of Delos, the handmaids of Him who shoots darts from a
    distance.
160 When they have first celebrated with hymnody[5] Phoebus Apollo,
Artemis also, dispenser of arrows, and Leto, their mother,
Then, in remembrance of men and of women of times long gone by,
    they
Sing a melodious hymn and enchant all the nations of mankind,
For they know well how to mimic the voices and chatter of all men;

---

5. The composition and singing of hymns or odes to and about the immortal gods, as here.

Anyone hearing them sing would declare he himself was the speaker,   165
So the articulate whole of their beautiful ode hangs together.
Come, then, Apollo, be kind, and propitious Artemis also.
Hail and farewell to you, maidens, remember me kindly hereafter
When anybody of humans on earth, say, a wayfaring stranger
Come to this island, should ask your opinion and pose you this   170
   question,
"Who, do you think, is the man that is sweetest of singers, O maidens,
Of those that visit you here? And in which do you take the most
   pleasure?"
Answer him then well together, unanimously in my favor:
"He is a blind man whose home is on Chios, that rugged and
   rockbound
Island, and all of his poems are excellent, now and hereafter."   175
I shall bear your reputation as far as I wander in circles
Over the earth to the fairly inhabited cities of men, who
Will be convinced and believe, for indeed it is truth that I tell them.
Nor shall I ever cease hymning Apollo, the long-distance archer,
Him of the silvery bow, whom the lovely-haired Leto gave birth to.   180

To Pythian Apollo

1   Master, the kingdom of Lycia, lovely Maeonia also,
With the desirable maritime town of Miletus are yours, and
You are the ruler perforce of the wave-splattered island of Delos.
Playing his lute he is going, the son of respectable Leto,
5   Plucking the elegant zither, to rocky and difficult Pytho,
Wearing ambrosial clothes permeated with incense; his lyre
Under his plectrum of gold makes metallic and ravishing music.
Next from the earth he ascends to Olympus as quick as a thought and
Enters the palace of Zeus and the gathering of other gods there.
10 No time at all, and the lyre and the lyric engage the immortals!
All of the Muses together, their beautiful voices in concert,
Hymn the ambrosial gifts of the gods, and the hardships of mankind
Such as men have to endure at the hands of the gods that are deathless
Since we live senseless and helpless, completely unable to even
15 Find a specific for death or a means of defense against old age.
Meanwhile, the Graces with beautiful hair, the benevolent Hours,
Join with Harmonia, Hebe, the daughter of Zeus, Aphrodite,
In the melodious dance, holding each others' hands by the wrist. And
One among these, not the least nor the worst of performers there is, but
20 Rather, exceedingly grand in appearance, of excellent beauty,
Artemis, strewer of arrows, the nurse-mate of Phoebus Apollo.
With them does Ares as well as the sharp-sighted slayer of Argus
Sport, while Apollo keeps time with the tune that he plays on the zither,
Highly and handsomely prancing, a radiance shining about him—
25 Sparks seem to glance from his feet and to glow in his close-woven
     tunic.
Leto, whose locks are of gold, and omniscient Zeus in his wisdom,
Watching him, please their magnanimous minds and delight their
     hearts greatly
At their adorable son blithely playing among the immortals.
How shall I hymn you, indeed, who are everywhere so celebrated?

Shall I describe you in love, in the arms of your lovers, describing 30
How as a wooer you went to the maidenly daughter of Azan
At the same time as brave Ischys, the son of Eliatus, the well horsed?
Or else with Phorbas, the offspring of Triops, or with Ereutheus?
Or with Leucippus, perhaps, and the wife of Leucippus? Who went on
Foot, and another on horseback, and didn't give up before Triops? 35
Or shall I tell how at first, in your search for a suitable spot in
Which to establish your oracle for all mankind, you descended,
Long-Distance Marksman, to earth and, immediately leaving Olympus,
Went to Pieria, passing by way of the sand banks of Lectus
And Aenianes and through the Perrhaebi? You came to Iolcus 40
Soon, and set foot on Cenaeon, in nautically famous Euboea,
Stood on the plain of Lelantus: it simply did not suit your humor
There to construct a great temple and grove full of various timber.
Thence passing over Euripus, you, accurate archer, Apollo,
Went up the holy green mountain; departing from which, you 45
    continued
To Mycalessus, and on to Teumessus, embedded in grassland.
Next did you visit the townsite of Thebes, still mantled in forest:
No one at that time—no mortal—inhabited Thebes's holy city,
Nor any paths whatsoever or ways were there, then, to approach it
Over the grain-growing plain about Thebes, for the forest possessed it. 50
Thence you proceeded, Apollo, O accurate long-distance archer,
Until you came to Onchestus, the glorious grove of Poseidon,
Wherein an unbroken colt catches breath—he is taxed to the utmost,
Drawing the beautiful carriage; his excellent driver, however,
Leaps from the car to the ground and proceeds on his way, while the 55
    horses,
Rid of authority, make the unoccupied vehicle rattle,
And, if they shatter the car in the midst of the tree-crowded thicket,
Then they abandon the thing on its side; but men look to the horses.
Such was the rite from the very beginning: they pray to their master;
As for the chariot, then it becomes the divinity's portion. 60

Thence you proceeded, Apollo, O accurate long-distance marksman,
Until you came to the stream of the beautiful, limpid Cephisus,
Which from Lilaea debouches its beautiful current of water.
This you traversed, and Ochalea next, with its numerous towers, our
65 Guard from afar, and you came to the meadowland round Haliartus.
Onward you went to Telphousa, inviolate place, where it suited
You to establish a temple and grove full of foliate bowers.
Standing right next to Telphousa herself, you addressed her this
    sentence,
"This is the place where, Telphousa, I mean to establish a temple,
70 Beautiful in the extreme, an oracular shrine for all mankind,
And to this spot will they always bring hecatombs such as are perfect,
Some of them those that inhabit the plenteous Peloponnesus,
Others the dwellers in Europe and islands encircled by water,
Coming in quest of an oracle. Prophecies shall I deliver,
75 Giving infallible counsel to all in my prosperous temple."
Such were the words with which Phoebus Apollo laid out the
    foundations,
Wide and extremely extensive throughout. When she saw this,
    Telphousa
Soon was provoked into anger and uttered the following statement:
"Distant protector, Lord Phoebus, I mean to appeal to your feelings,
80 Since you are thinking of building a gorgeously beautiful temple
Here, which will be an oracular shrine for mankind, who will always
Come bringing with them immaculate hecatombs meant for your
    worship.
What I shall say to you, nevertheless, do you take to your bosom.
You will be always annoyed by the noise of the swift-footed horses,
85 Also the mules that are watered as well at my sacrosanct sources.
Here, any one of mankind might prefer to examine the well-wrought
Chariots and would attend to the noise of the swift-footed horses
More than your grandiose temple and all the possessions within it.
Lord, if you listen to me for a bit, inasmuch as you are both

Bigger and better than I, and your strength, of the two, is the greater,   90
You should construct it in Crisa, a hollow beneath Mount Parnassus:
There will no beautiful chariots whirl to distract you, nor noise of
Swift-footed horses will there be about your well-located altar;
But, as the better known tribes of mankind bring you offerings, as the
Healer invoked in the paean, then, thoroughly cheered in your feelings,   95
You will receive pretty ritual gifts from the peoples about you."
So she declared, and persuaded the heart of the long distance archer,
Unto this end, that renown in that region belong to Telphousa,
Not to the archer. And thence you proceeded, O far-flung Apollo,
Further, and came to the town of the violent Phlegyan people,   100
Who, being utterly careless of Zeus, are inhabitants, on earth,
Of a most beautiful vale in the neighborhood of Lake Cephisus.
Next, at a furious rate, off you rushed to the ridge of the mountain
Range: unto Crisa you came, in the shadow of snowy Parnassus,
Crisa, a shoulder of rock that is turned to the west, while above, a   105
Precipice hangs, and a hollow ravine runs along underneath it,
Rugged and steep; and there Phoebus Apollo, the master, determined
He should construct his delectable temple and made this
     pronouncement:
"Here do I purpose to build my exceedingly beautiful dwelling
As an oracular place of resort for mankind, who will always   110
Come bringing with them immaculate hecatombs meant for my
     pleasure—
Peoples who people the plentiful region of Peloponnesus,
Also the dwellers in Europe and over the sea-circled islands,
Seeking my prophecies: them shall I treat to infallible counsel,
Giving oracular answers to all in my opulent temple."   115
When he had spoken, Apollo began to lay out the foundations,
Broad and extremely extensive throughout. And upon these foundations,
Later, Trophonius and Agamedes, the sons of Erginus,
Put down a threshold of stone—men beloved of the gods that are
     deathless.

120 Round this anonymous hordes of humans constructed a temple
　　Made out of masonry, which shall be sung of for ever and ever.
　　Nearby, a beautiful fountain flowed: this was the spot where the Master,
　　Leto's son, slew with his powerful bow the formidable dragon.
　　It was a female, immense and well nourished and savage, a monster
125 That had done plentiful harm upon earth unto humans, both them and
　　Also their neat-footed sheep; a great bane she was, a bloody nuisance.
　　Furthermore, she had accepted from Hera, whose throne is of gold,
　　　　dread
　　Typhon to nurse, a vexatious and terrible pest unto mortals,
　　Whom Hera bore at a time she was angry with Zeus, the begetter,
130 Since the descendant of Cronus gave birth to distinguished Athena
　　Out of his head; whereupon Lady Hera waxed suddenly wroth and
　　Uttered the following speech to the gods that were gathered together:
　　"Listen to me, all you gods, and you goddesses also, and hear how
　　Zeus, the collector of clouds, is beginning to treat with dishonor
135 Me, whom he once made his wife on account of my excellent
　　　　knowledge.
　　Now he has—quite independent of me—given birth to the owl-eyed
　　One, who, indeed, is outstanding among all the blessed immortals.
　　As for my baby, Hephaestus, the child I gave birth to myself, he
　　Is a conspicuous weakling among all the gods and a cripple.
140 Picking him up in my arms, I rejected him into the deep sea;
　　Thetis, however, the daughter of Nereus, silvery-footed
　　Thetis received him, and she with her sisters the nymphs entertained
　　　　him.
　　Better that she had devised something else to make merry the blessed
　　Gods! Now, you quick-witted scoundrel, what mischief do you propose
　　　　further?
145 How could you—how did you dare—be delivered of owl-eyed Athena?
　　Wouldn't I do, as a mother? And yet I was called, was I not, your
　　Wife in the company of the immortals who occupy heaven?
　　Careful now, lest I conceive something awful for you in the future!

Now I shall hit on a practical method whereby may be born my
Son who is going to show as a prodigy with the immortals,   150
Without dishonoring your sacred bed or my own reputation.
Nor do I mean to frequent your embraces, but rather, without you,
Keeping myself at a distance, consort with the other immortals."
When she had spoken, she went far away from the gods, being angry.
Striking the ground with the flat of her hand, Lady Hera, the cow-eyed   155
Goddess, orated as follows and uttered the following prayer.
"Listen to me now, you earth, and broad heaven extending above earth!
Also you Titans, divinities of subterranean habits,
Dwellers in Tartarus, whence are descended the gods and all humans:
All of you, listen to my imprecation, and give me a baby   160
Born without Zeus, but in no way deficient in strength to his father:
Let him be just as much stronger as wide-viewing Zeus is than Cronus!"
Voicing this prayer, she walloped the earth with the flat of her hand, and
Earth, the sustainer of life, was excited to movement—which seeing,
Hera rejoiced in her will, for she thought that it would be accomplished. 165
Thenceforth, thereafter, until the accomplishment of a whole year, she
Never did go to the couch of the counselor, Zeus, neither sat, as
Once was her wont, on her throne with its intricate workmanship, ever
Shrewdly devising, as heretofore, clever and closely laid counsel.
Rather, remaining at home in her prayerful and popular temples,   170
Hera, majestic and ox eyed, delighted in ritual worship.
But when the months and the days were accomplished that had been
     appointed,
And, in a year's revolution the seasons were come to fulfillment,
Hera gave birth to a creature resembling neither the gods nor
Humans, a troublesome, terrible nuisance to men, namely, Typhon.   175
Taking this offspring of hers, then, majestical Hera, the ox eyed,[6]
Brought him and gave him, at once, as one pest, to another; the dragon

6. Large, bovine eyes were a mark of beauty in women; "cow-eyed" would sound too
much like "cowhide."

Welcomed the child, who inflicted much wrong on respectable
    mankind.
If a man met with this dragon, the day of his death was upon him,
180 Until Apollo, the long-distance archer, let fly a strong arrow,
So that the monster lay wracked by intolerable physical anguish,
Mightily panting and rolling about on the ground in a frenzy;
Her supernatural voice grew in volume unspeakably awful,
Thickly she writhed through the wood, rolling this way and that, till she
    let her
185 Murderous spirit escape with her breath; then Apollo exulted,
"There let you rot where you lie, on the earth that gives food unto
    humans!
No more a mischievous bane will you be as you were in your lifetime,
For mortal men who are fed on the fruit of all-nourishing earth and
Who to this spot will come bringing immaculate hecatombs with them.
190 Neither will Typhon against ineluctable death be protection,
Nor the Chimaera, in spite of her terrible name, but the black earth
Here and the radiant heat of Hyperion will make you rotten."
Thus he exulted, and utterly darkness occluded her eyes, and
Soon had the sun with his sacred intensity rendered her rotten;
195 Therefore, the place to this day is called Pytho, or "rotten," and people
Call the Lord Phoebus, as well, by this title of Pythian, seeing
There it was Helios's piercing intensity rotted the monster.
Presently, Phoebus Apollo perceived and was inwardly certain
Wherein the fluent and beautiful fountain had wished to deceive him.
200 Straight to Telphousa he went in his anger, and soon he approached her;
Standing exceedingly close to her side, he addressed her as follows:
"You were not meant to obtain, by distracting my purpose, Telphousa,
This lovely land as your own, to pour through it your fair, flowing
    waters.
My reputation, as well, shall be here, and not only your own fame."
205 Then did the marksman Apollo thrust forward a chunk of the
    mountain,

Loosing a torrent of stones so he covered the course of the spring and
There, in the midst of her tree-crowded grove, he constructed his altar
Next to the beautiful site of the copious source; for this reason,
Everyone prays to the Lord as "Telphousian," using this title
Since he at one time dishonored the waters of sacred Telphousa.   210
Presently, Phoebus Apollo consulted his heart and considered
What sort of men he should gather together as ministers, both to
Serve him and sacrifice unto his cult in precipitous Pytho.
As he was pondering thus, he perceived on the wine-colored sea a
Swift sailing vessel, and men were within her, both many and noble,   215
Cretans from Knossos, the city of Minos, who now for the Master
Rightly perform all the rites and deliver the lawful decrees of
Phoebus Apollo, whose sword is of gold, with the oracles which he
Speaks from his laurel that grows in the valleys beneath Mount
    Parnassus.
Then, they were sailing toward sandy Pylos and all of its natives,   220
Bent upon rapine and plunder, and black was the vessel that bore them.
Phoebus Apollo, however, encountered them as they were sailing.
Out of the water he leapt in the likeness and shape of a dolphin
Onto the swift-moving ship, where he lay, a huge monster and horrid.
Anyone then of the sailors who took it in mind to eject him   225
Roughly he shook all about as he shivered the beams of the vessel.
So all the pirates in silence sat trembling, so terribly frightened
None of them moved to unfasten the rigging that hung on the hollow
Ship, nor to lower the sail of the boat with its navy-blue bowsprit.
But as they first had attached all the canvas with tendons of ox hide,   230
So they continued to sail further; briskly behind them a south wind
Stirred the swift ship. And they rounded Cape Malea first on their route,
    and
Cruised the Laconian coastline, a country encircled by sea, and
Passing the country of Helios, he who gives pleasure to mortals,
Came to Taenarum, the place where the fat, fleecy sheep of the sun god,   235
Helios, pasture forever—and that is a ravishing region!

There they desired to anchor their ship and perhaps disembark to
Watch if they might comprehend this great marvel and see with their
    own eyes
Whether the monster would stay on the deck of the elegant vessel
240 Or would jump back in the salty and fish-swarming element round it.
Then was the finely made ship disobedient unto her helmsman;
Keeping the opulent Peloponnesus, however, on one hand,
Onward she sped on her way. Lord Apollo, the long-distance archer,
Easily guided her straight with the breeze, and, pursuing her route, she
245 Passed by Arena and passed by attractive Argyphea, quickly
Speeding past Thryon, the ford of the Alpheus, nicely placed Aipu,
And sandy Pylos, as well as the men that are native to Pylos.
Further she went, past the Cruni and Chalcis, and thither past Dyme,
Finally leaving behind brilliant Elis, controlled by the Epei.
250 As they were casting for Phera and glad of a fair wind from heaven,
Under the clouds there appeared to them Ithaca's upstanding
    mountain,
Same appeared, and Dulichium also, and woody Zacynthus;
But when at last they had passed by the whole of the Peloponnesus,
In the direction of Crisa appeared the unlimited inlet
255 Which interrupts through the midst of its width the rich island of
    Pelops.
Came a great blast of a freshening west wind, at Zeus's injunction,
Boisterous, blowing from heaven, in order that quickly as might be
This little ship could accomplish its course through the sea's salty water.
Afterward, backward they turned, toward morning, and sailed to the
    sun with
260 Zeus's son Phoebus Apollo, the master, as guide and commander,
Until they came into Crisa, a sunny and vine-bearing spot, and
Into the harbor: the sea-going ship ran aground on the sandbar.
Out of the vessel, Apollo, the master who wards from a distance,
Leapt, like a star in the midst of the day, and a myriad flashes
265 Flew from his person, the brilliance of which mounted up into heaven.

Passing the valuable tripods, he entered the depths of his temple,
Where, manifesting the shafts of his might, he enkindled a flash fire:
Brightness enveloped all Crisa, and loudly the Crisean women
Set up a wailing, the wives and the daughters, so handsomely girdled,
Under the impulse of Phoebus, who cast into each a great terror.   270
Out of the temple he leapt like a thought, and he sped to the vessel,
Taking the likeness and shape of a vigorous, powerful hero
In his first youth, who was wearing his hair falling over his shoulders.
Lifting his voice, he addressed wingèd words to the men in the vessel.
"Strangers, who are you, and whence do you sail on the watery   275
    highroad?
After some plunder, perhaps, or at random indeed do you wander
Over the sea, in the manner of pirates, whose way is to wander,
Risking their lives to bring mischief to strangers of foreign extraction?
Why are you sitting so glum? For you neither are going ashore nor
Stowing away the equipment and rigging all over your black ship.   280
It is but right for such seafaring men as must work for a living,
When they would put into shore from the deep in their dark-painted
    vessel,
Weary and worn with exertion, at once to be seized with exhaustion;
Hunger grips hold of their guts and a wish for delicious refreshment."
Such was the speech by which Phoebus put courage in everyone's   285
    bosom.
When he had spoken, the chief of the Cretans addressed him in answer,
"Stranger, although you in no way resemble us men, who must perish,
Either in form or in stature, but rather the gods that are deathless,
Health and great joy to you also: I pray that the gods give you blessings!
Now, will you tell me the truth about this, so I know it for certain: 290
What is this region—what country?—and who are the people that live
    here?
Having in mind somewhere else did we sail the great gulf of the ocean,
Heading for Pylos from Crete, of which country we boast ourselves
    natives.

Yet in our ship we are come other ways, altogether unwilling,
295 Settled, indeed, on return, and a different route altogether.
Nevertheless, an immortal has brought us, though we did not wish it."
Then did Apollo, the long-distance guardian, speak out in answer.
"Foreigners, who used to dwell all about thickly forested Knossos
Previously, but who never again will return any more to
300 Either your lovely city, nor, any of you, to your own homes
Or your dear wives, but shall live on the site of my opulent temple
Here as its keepers, for it will be honored by many of mankind,
I am the scion of Zeus; I declare I indeed am Apollo,
And it is I who have brought you here over the sea's great abysses,
305 Meaning no evil indeed. For, moreover, you will be the keepers
Here of this opulent temple of mine, highly honored of mankind,
Knowing the counsels of those that are deathless, and at our discretion
You shall have honor forever, the rest of your days without ending.
Come, and as quickly as possible, see you obey as I tell you.
310 First, you must lower the sail and unfasten the riggings of leather,
Then you must draw up your swift sailing ship on the beach above tide
    line;
Take your possessions and everything else in the even ship out and
With them erect at the edge of the sea, where the waves break, an altar.
Kindle a fire upon it for sacrifice, offering barley.
315 Thereupon, you are to utter a prayer as you stand round the altar.
And, insofar as at first from the depths of the dark misty sea I
Leapt on your swift sailing ship in the likeness and form of a dolphin,
So you must pray unto Delphic Apollo, 'the Lord of the Dolphin';
Also, my altar shall always be Delphic as well as all-seeing.
320 Afterward, make and partake of your evening meal by the black ship,
Pouring libations to all of the gods that inhabit Olympus.
But when you have put away all desire for delicious refreshment,
Singing the hymn to the healer, the paean, accompany me till
Soon you arrive at the place where you will keep my opulent temple."
325 Such was his sentence. They hearkened, and generously they obeyed him.

Taking the sail down, at first they unfastened the rigging of cowhide;
When they had lowered the mast by its stays into resting position,
They disembarked on the beach, on the edge of the sea, where the waves
    break.
Out of the water they dragged their swift ship up the beach past the tide
    line,
Over the sand, and extended long stays at its side to support it.   330
Then, at the edge of the sea where the waves break, they fashioned an
    altar,
Kindling a fire upon it for sacrifice, offering barley,
Praying as he had commanded them to as they stood round the altar.
Afterward, they took their supper beside the swift, black-painted vessel,
Pouring libations to each of the Blest that inhabit Olympus.   335
Then, when they had put away all desire for food and for drink, they
Went on their way, and the Master, Apollo, Zeus's son, was their leader,
Holding his lyre in his hands as he strummed in an elegant manner,
Highly and handsomely prancing along, and they followed him,
    dancing,
Singing the hymn to the Healer, "O Paean," those Cretans, to Pytho.   340
Such are the paean-performers of Crete, also those whom the goddess
Muse has infused, through and through, with the voice of melodious
    music.
Thus they proceeded, on foot and unwearied, until they had reached the
Ridge and arrived pretty soon at Parnassus, delectable spot where
Phoebus was going to dwell, highly honored by many of mankind.   345
Guidelike, he showed them his numinous shrine and his opulent
    temple.
Spirit, however, bestirred in the innermost hearts of the Cretans,
So that their leader demanded an answer, and asked of Apollo:
"Since you have brought us away from our dear ones and far from our
    homeland,
Master, for such was the journey that somehow seemed best to your   350
    purpose,

How are we going to live now? This much we are prompted to ask you,
Seeing this region desirable neither for vineyard nor pasture,
So that one might make a comfortable livelihood here and serve men
    too."
Smiling upon them, Apollo, the scion of Zeus, thus addressed them:
355 "Foolish are men, and long-suffering too, inasmuch as you wish for
Grievous and cumbersome labors, and straits, and vexation of spirit.
Easily shall I impose on your wits with the tale I shall tell you:
Even if every one of you, taking a knife in his right hand,
Slaughtered the sheep here incessantly, there would remain an
    abundance,
360 Such the supply the respectable peoples of mankind will bring me!
Serve as the guard of my temple and welcome the nations of mankind
Gathered together at Delphi; especially heed my directions,
Show them to mortals. Accept my decrees as the guide of your
    conscience.
But if some meaningless word should occur, or some frivolous action,
365 Violent arrogance too, as seems just among men, who must perish,
Others than you shall hereafter be masters and guides and directors,
Whom of necessity you shall be subject to daily forever.
Everything now has been said; see you guard it securely within you."
So it is! Hail and Farewell to you, scion of Zeus and of Leto,
370 Presently, I shall remember another about you, and sing it.

IV. TO HERMES

Muse, sing a hymn about Hermes, the infant of Zeus and of Maia,   1
Governor over Cyllene and pastoral Arcady also,
Light-fingered messenger of the immortals, whom Maia gave birth to—
Bashful and lovely-haired nymph, who had mingled in liking with great
    Zeus.
Shunning the company of all the blest, she inhabited some deep   5
Shadowy cavern, where Zeus in the dead of the night would consort to
Mingle his substance with that of the lovely-haired nymph when he
    thought that
Pleasant repose overwhelmed white-armed Hera, his sister and wife,
    thus
Fooling the undying gods, fooling men who are born but to perish.
But when the purpose of almighty Zeus was accomplished in heaven,   10
And the tenth month was appointed for Maia, then Zeus brought it all
    to
Light, so their doings were manifest. Then she gave birth to a baby,
Devious, wily, a robber, a rustler of cattle, a dream guide—
Yes, the conductor of dreams—and a spy in the night, and a lookout
Skulking at other men's doors, who was presently going to show off   15
Glorious deeds and notorious doings among the immortals.
Born in the morning, by noon he was playing the zither, by nightfall
He had abducted the cattle belonging to marksman Apollo,
On the fourth day of the month, the day Maia, the ladylike, bore him.
When he had sprung from the undying womb of his mother, not very   20
Long did he linger abed in his ritual basketwork cradle;

Rather, he leapt up in search of the cattle of Phoebus Apollo.
As he was passing out over the threshold, before the high-ceilinged
Cave he discovered a tortoise, from which he derived much delight, for
25 Hermes it was who originally made the tortoise a singer.
She first encountered her maker in front of the gate of the forecourt,
Where she was browsing upon the luxuriant grass at the house front,
Swaying along on four feet. How the light-fingered grandson of Cronus
Laughed when he noticed the tortoise, immediately saying as follows,
30 "Omen to me so propitious already, I shall not despise you!
Greetings, my graceful, desirable chorister, banquet companion!
Welcome, well-met apparition! Now where did you get that fine
      plaything?
I mean, your colorful shell? You, a tortoise that lives in the mountains?
Picking you up, I will carry you into the house. You will be of
35 Use to me, yet I intend no dishonor; but first you shall serve me.
Better to be in the house: out of doors it is dangerous for you.
You shall be during your life a defense against mischievous magic,
And if you happen to die, you will sing very beautifully after."
When he had spoken, in both of his hands he immediately lifted
40 Up the adorable plaything and carried it into the house, where,
Flipping it onto its back, he began with a knife of gray iron
Neatly to scrape out the vitals of that mountain-frequenting tortoise.
As when a rapid idea transfixes the breast of a man whom
Cares thick and fast have obsessed and encircled, or when from the
      rolling
45 Eyes coruscations dart glancing—so quickly did honorable Hermes
Hit on the deed realized simultaneous with its conception.
Fastening sections of reed, which he'd fashioned according to measure,
Over the back where he'd pierced through the tortoiseshell, tightly he
      stretched the
Skin of a bull over all; with congenital practical know-how,
50 Setting the horns in position, he fitted the bridge in between them,
Stretching the seven harmonious strings he had made out of sheep gut.

When he completed its structure, he took the desirable plaything,
Tuning it first with a plectrum; it gave forth a wonderful music
Under his touch. Then the god very beautifully sang to his own sweet
Improvisation, like boys, adolescents, on festive occasions,   55
Bandying sly innuendo. He sang about Zeus, son of Cronus,
And about Maia, the prettily sandaled, and how they consorted
Once in the friendship of love, and he told of his proper conception
And of his honorable name, and he spelled it all out in some detail,
Next celebrating the servants and glorious home of the nymph, the   60
Tripods as well as the plentiful cauldrons that furnished her household.
These were the matters he sang; while at heart he was thinking of
     others.
Taking the hollowed-out lyre, he laid it away in his holy
Wickerwork cradle, and, hankering after fresh meat, he ascended
Out of the sweet-smelling hall to a place of advantage, a lookout,   65
Pondering utter deceit in his heart, such as brigands and robbers
Make their professional care under cover of colorless night. The
Sun was descending from earth into ocean with horses and car when
Hermes arrived at a run at the shady Pierian mountains,
Where the ambrosial cattle belonging to blessed immortals   70
Kept to their byres and pastured upon the unmown, lovely meadows.
Of these, the infant of Maia, the keen-sighted slayer of Argus,
Cutting off fifty loud-bellowing cows from the herd, quickly drove them
Every which way over sandy terrain, thus confusing their footprints;
And he remembered another deceitful technique, for he turned their   75
Hoofprints about, with the front ones behind and the back ones in
     front, while
Walking the opposite way. Then he wove himself wickerwork sandals
Out of the reeds in the sand of the seashore: a marvelous work not
Mentioned before, neither thought of, of tamarisk branches and myrtle
Twigs intermingled. He tied the green wood in a bundle beneath his   80
Feet and attached them securely and comfortably, foliage and all:
Such were the delicate sandals the glorious slayer of Argus

Plucked for his journey and made in Pieria, like someone getting
Ready to take a long trip in a rather original fashion.

85 Recognized by an old man who was ditching his flowering vineyard
As he was hurrying over the plain toward grassy Onchestus,
Him then the son of respectable Maia forthrightly addressed thus:
"Granddad, your shoulders are bent as you dig round the roots of your garden,
Yet when the vineyard bears fruit at last, yours is a copious vintage.

90 Seeing, pretend to be blind, and be deaf though you've certainly heard me:
Silence! If nothing belonging to you has been anyway damaged."
When he'd concluded this warning, he hurried the strong herd of cattle
All in a bunch over many a shadowy mountain and valley
Noisy with echoes; he drove them across many flowering prairies.

95 When supernatural night, his mysterious ally, was nearly
Over, and soon would the sunrise begin to set people to labor,
When bright Selene,[7] the daughter of Pallas, son of Magamedes,
Mounted her lookout anew: to the Alpheus river came Zeus's son,
Driving before him the beetle-browed cattle of Phoebus Apollo.

100 Up to the lofty-roofed shelter before an egregious meadow
Trotted the cattle, unyoked, uncompelled, to their troughs and their mangers.
When he had handsomely fed them on fodder, the loud-lowing cattle
Hermes drove into the barn in a bunch; there he left them to browse on
Clover and galingale covered with dew. He collected a heap of

105 Dry wood, kindling and logs, and invented the science of fire.
Taking a glistening faggot of laurel, he trimmed it with iron,
Fitted it into his palm, and the hot breath of fire was awakened.
Hermes thus, first of all, furnished the trappings of fire, and fire.
Into a deeply dug trench, he put plenty of beautiful kindling,

110 Dry and abundant and thick. Far away, the conspicuous flame flashed,

7. The moon.

Casting a terrible blast from the blaze of the crackling bonfire.
Then, while the force of Hephaestus was causing the fire to kindle,
Out of the barn famous Hermes had taken two crooked-horned cattle,
Leading them, lowing aloud, to the fire: such capacity filled him!
Throwing them down on the ground on their backs and then rolling   115
    them over,
When he had pulled them about and they lay out of breath, he
    transfixed their
Vitals. Performing one task then another, he cut off the fatty
Rich meat, roasting it spitted on sticks cut of wood, all together,
Flesh and the parts of the carcass reserved for the gods, and the black
    blood
Wrapped in the entrails as sausage; the rest he left lying in situ.   120
Over a steep ragged rock he extended the hides of the cattle;
There, very old, an unthinkable time after all this, they still are.
After high-spirited Hermes had lifted his handiwork, dripping,
Onto a slippery slab, he divided it into twelve portions
Strictly according to lot, and a perfectly honorable piece he   125
Laid at each place. He desired the meats of the sacrifice greatly,
Honorable Hermes! The smell of them tickled his undying nostrils,
Sweet as it was, but his masterful mind was not swayed thereby, very
Eager albeit he was to devour the sacred refreshments.
Rather, he laid up the edible parts in the lofty-roofed byre,   130
Fat and the plentiful meat, and immediately hung them on high, as
Clues to his fresh depredation. Then piling dry wood on the bonfire,
All of the hoofs and the horns he completely destroyed in the hot
    flames.
When the divinity finished his business according to schedule,
Into the rapid, deep-flowing Alpheus he cast off his sandals,   135
Dampened the embers, and carefully covered with sand all the black
    ash,
Spending the rest of the night while the beautiful light of Selene
Shone down. Hermes returned to the glittering heights of Cyllene

Soon, as the sun was just rising, and no one encountered him in the
140 Course of his journey, no blessed immortal or man born to perish,
No barking dogs. But the light-fingered offspring of Zeus, noble
    Hermes,
Slipping in sideways by way of the keyhole, crept into the great hall,
Taking the shape of a breeze of late summer or watery vapor.
Straight through the cavern he went till he came to the opulent alcove,
145 Swiftly advancing on tiptoe; the floor did not ring to his footfall.
Quickly he crept to his wickerwork cradle, respectable Hermes!
Pulling the swaddling bands over his shoulders, he lay like an infant
New born, playfully feeling the blanket that bunched round his knees,
    but
Keeping his darling, the tortoiseshell, well within reach on his right side.
150 Nor was his mother, the goddess, deceived by the god, and she said so.
"What is the meaning of—? where have you been at this hour of the
    night?—eh?
Crafty and subtle and cloaked in audacity, well do I know you
Soon will be hauled out of doors at the hands of indignant Apollo,
Bound with impossible bonds round your waist. Or perhaps in the
    meanwhile
155 Off you will go on your own to behave like a thief in the mountain
Glens? Go back where you came from! Your father begot you, a worry
Both to the undying gods and to men, who are born but to perish."
Hermes returned to his mother a cunningly worded reply, "Dear
Mother, how can you upbraid me as if I were only a newborn
160 Baby that knows precious little, at my age, of evil affections,
Trembling, fearful of nothing so much as a parent's reproaches?
I shall embrace a profession, whichever is best to provide us—
You and myself—with a living, infallibly: keep us in clover!
Nor shall we meekly endure here, as you would suggest that we ought to,
165 Staying at home, of all gods the least honored by gifts and by prayers.
Better the rest of our days to sit gossiping with the immortals,
Rich and important as landowners, than to inhabit this drafty

Cavern: our home! In regard to the matter of *honor* and *worship*:
I shall embark on Religion, like Phoebus Apollo, my brother.
And if my father forbids it, I yet shall achieve the ambition   170
That I am capable of, namely, being the chief of the robbers.
So, should the son of respectable Leto come looking for me, I
Think he will find something different, more than he bargained to meet
    with.
For I am going to Pytho to burgle his sizable temple,
Where I shall plunder sufficient surpassingly beautiful tripods,   175
Cauldrons, and gold in abundance, and plenty of glittering iron,
Many fine clothes in addition, which you shall behold if you wish to."
Such were the words they employed in conversing together, the son of
Goatskin-shield-brandishing Zeus and his mother, the ladylike Maia.
Dawn, morning's daughter, who brings to mankind, who must die,   180
    illustration,
Rose from the depths of the river of Ocean, as Phoebus Apollo,
Traveling, came to the very delectable grove of Onchestus,
Sacred to earth-shaking, loud-voiced Poseidon. He found there an old
    man
Grazing a beast at the roadside, a jackass, the prop of his vineyard.
Him, then, the son of respectable Leto forthrightly addressed thus: 185
"Grandfather, plucker of brambles, from grassy Pieria I've come
Seeking the cattle, all cows and all crooked of horn, separated
Out of my herd. Now the coal-colored bull grazed apart from the others
All by himself, but the bright-eyed dogs were protecting the stragglers,
Four of them all of one mind, nearly human! The bull and the dogs   190
    were
Left—which is almost incredible! Just after sunset, the cows went
Forth from the delicate meadow and quit their delectable pasture.
Grandfather born a long time ago, please tell me this: have you noticed
Anyone passing this way—any man—with these cattle before him?"
Then the old fellow addressed him and answered his question in these   195
    words,

"My dear boy, it's a difficult task to describe everything that
Anyone's eyes may behold. Many wayfarers travel this highway,
Some of them meaning much evil and others intending some good; they
Pass to and fro, and it's hard to examine each one. And, moreover,
200 I had been digging all day round the slope of my vineyard, till sunset,
There, where it's richest in wine. But I think that I noticed, your honor,
Though I'm not certain, a boy—or whoever he was—a mere infant,
Following after some handsome-horned cattle; he carried a wand and
Walked back and forth; he was driving the cattle the wrong way about so
205 Somehow they seemed to go backward while keeping their heads to
    their drover."
So the old man. After hearing his story, Apollo began to
Press on his way. When he noticed a narrow-winged bird,[8] he inferred at
Once that the thief was the infant engendered of Zeus, son of Cronus.
Zeus's son, lordly Apollo, was off and away in a flash to
210 Excellent Pylos in search of his round-footed, waddling cattle,
Wrapping about his broad shoulders a cloak of a cloud-colored-
    crimson.
When he examined the hoofprints, the Dealer of Death from Afar said,
"Goodness! but this is a miracle which I behold with my own eyes.
Here are the hoofprints quite clearly belonging to cattle with straight
    horns,
215 Strangely reversed so they're pointed again to the asphodel meadow.
Yet these are never the footprints belonging to man or to woman,
No more to gray-coated wolves or to bears, nor the footprints of lions,
Nor do I think they are anything proper to shaggy-maned centaurs.
Who can it be that advancing on ravenous feet makes such monstrous
220 Tracks—on this side of the road pretty queer, and much worse on the
    other?"
Speaking, the master, Apollo, Zeus's son, lightly sped on his way and

---

8. Compare Hesiod, *Works and Days*, 201–10; perhaps the hawk, as a raptor, was as-
sociated with rapacious Hermes.

Came to the Mount of Cyllene, its slopes thickly mantled with forests,
Into a shady deep hollow of rock where ambrosial Maia
Had been delivered of Hermes, Zeus's son and the grandson of Cronus.
Sweet was the odor diffused everywhere through the excellent   225
    mountain;
Many, the narrow-hoofed sheep that were grazing upon the green grass
    there.
There, at that time, in a hurry descended across the stone lintel
Into the vaporous cavern Apollo, who shoots from a distance.
When he perceived the Far Shooter was furious over his cattle,
Into his sweet-smelling bedclothes the infant of Zeus and of Maia   230
Snuggled: so wood ash, in settling on plentiful embers, conceals them.
Hermes, on seeing the Guard from Afar, rolled himself in a ball and
Into a little contracted his head and his hands and his feet and
Lay like a newly breached baby that is seeking delicious repose, while
Actually vigilant, holding his tortoiseshell lyre in his armpit.   235
Phoebus Apollo perceived and did not fail to recognize either
Maia, the beautiful nymph of the mountain, or Hermes, her dear son,
Lying there like a small baby, while wrapped in the shifts of deception.
Peering about, up and down, into every recess of the great hall,
Taking a glittering key, he threw open three closets containing   240
Nectar and lovely ambrosia; plenty of gold and of silver
Lay there within, and abundance of crimson and silver-trimmed
    garments,
Maia the nymph's, of the sort that the holy abodes of the blessed
Goddesses always contain. When he'd thoroughly pried in the corners
All through the house, with these words Leto's son spoke to honorable   245
    Hermes.
"Child, lying low in your cradle, immediately show me my cattle,
Otherwise we two shall differ, and hardly according to order!
Catching you up, I shall cast you away into Tartarus's murky
Dark ineluctable, horrible doom! from which neither your mother
Nor Father Zeus shall release you that you may revisit the daylight: 250

Under the earth evermore you shall wander, the captain of Wee Folk."
Hermes replied to his brother, but cunningly worded his answer:
"What is the meaning of these cruel words, son of Leto, you utter?
Is it in search of your pastoral cattle you pay us this visit?
255 I have not seen them nor learned of them from the report of another.
Therefore, I cannot inform you, nor win the reward of informers.
Do I resemble a rustler of cattle—a muscular he-man?
This is no doing of mine; other matters have preoccupied me
Hitherto: sleep was my business, sleep and the milk of my mother,
260 Keeping the bedclothes tucked over my shoulders, and tepid ablutions.
Let no one learn whence this quarrel arose: it would be a great wonder,
Even among the immortals—an infant new born who has passed the
Courtyard with cows from the field? You are making extravagant
      charges!
I was born yesterday; my feet are sensitive to the uneven
265 Earth underfoot. If you wish, I will swear a great oath by my father's
Head: I insist I am neither, myself, the responsible party,
Nor have I seen anybody abducting your reverence's cattle—
'Cattle'—whatever that means! For I know of them only by hearsay."
When he had spoken, a twinkle escaped from his quick-rolling eyes as,
270 Raising his brows, he kept looking about him on this side and that and
Whistling under his breath, as if listening to a tall story.
Chuckling softly, Apollo, the Guardian far off, addressed him:
"Rascal, you devious trickster, I really believe that you have quite
Frequently entered, nocturnally, handsome inhabited houses,
275 Leaving full many a man to repose, if at all, on his bare floor,
Since you have stolen his furniture, and without making a sound: the
Way that you talk! Many pastoral shepherds in mountainous valleys
You will annoy with your craving for meat when you meet with their
      fleecy
Sheep or their cattle. Get out of that basketwork cradle this instant!
280 Come on, get up! Lest this nap be the ultimate sleep that you slumber,
Comrade of black night! This will be *your* reputation: hereafter,

You shall be called chief of brigands forever among the immortals."
When he had spoken, Apollo laid hold of the infant to lift him.
Meanwhile, the mighty destroyer of Argus considered a bit and,
Lifted in Phoebus's arms, he let fly an impertinent omen,   285
Namely a loud and presumptuous messenger, serf of the belly,[9]
Following quickly upon which he sneezed. When Apollo had heard this,
Instantly out of his arms to the ground he cast honorable Hermes.
Squatting in front of the child, although eager to be on his way, he
Taunted him mercilessly, with these words which he instantly uttered: 290
"Be of good cheer, little 'diapers,' the by-blow of Zeus and of Maia,
Presently I shall discover the whereabouts of all my cattle,
Thanks to these omens, and you shall yourself be my guide and
     detective."
Such was his speech; and now rapidly rose up Cyllenian Hermes;
Moving with speed, he enveloped himself to the neck in his bedclothes, 295
Clapping both hands to his ears as he uttered the following query,
"Where are you taking me, Warden? the maddest of all the immortals!
Is it because of your cows that you persecute me with such anger?
Goodness, I wish that the race of all kine were erased from the earth. I
Neither have stolen your cattle nor witnessed their theft by another: 300
'Cattle'—whatever that means, for I know of them only by hearsay.
Ask and accept the decision of Zeus, the successor of Cronus."
Hermes, the shepherd-to-be, and Latona's all-glorious offspring
Talked over everything thoroughly, both of them highly indignant.
Phoebus, by accurate speech, was entrapping respectable Hermes,   305
Not without cause, on the subject of cows; while the God of Cyllene
Wished to escape by his arts and his arguments silver-bowed Phoebus,
Finding, although he was full of resource, that the other had many
Matching devices. At last he set out in impetuous fashion
Over the sandy terrain, and his brother, Apollo, came after.   310
Soon to the summit of fragrant Olympus the beautiful children

9. He farted.

Came, to their father, the scion of Cronus, omnipotent King Zeus.
There was the balance of justice established for both the disputants.
There was a sociable murmur on snow-inundated Olympus,
315 Where the unwithered immortals had gathered not long after sunrise.
Hermes and Phoebus Apollo, the silver bowed, stood at the knees of
Zeus, the High Thunderer, who briefly asked of his dazzling firstborn,
"Phoebus, now where are you coming from, driving this excellent booty,
Namely, a newly born baby that nonetheless looks like a herald?
320 *This* is a serious matter to enter a godly assembly!"
Thus in reply the Far Guardian, lordly Apollo, addressed him,
"Father, if you will but listen, you shall hear no outmoded stories.
Though you reproach me for being the only one eager for booty,
This 'little boy' I discovered, and after an arduous journey,
325 Up near the top of Cyllene: a palpable, obvious burglar,
Yes, and a mocker whose like among gods I have never encountered,
Certainly not among men who mislead other men upon earth. He
Stole from their pasture my cattle and drove them at evening by the
Beach of the loud-roaring sea and directed their steps toward Pylos.
330 Double their tracks, truly monstrous, and such as to make someone
wonder,
Clearly the work of a bright, supernatural agent of parts; for,
As for the cows, the black dust made apparent their hoofprints, but
going
Backward, it seemed, to the asphodel meadow; while as for himself, he
Walked upon neither his hands nor his feet—an impossible feat and
335 Incomprehensible—over the sandy terrain: by some other
Means had he worn such a curious path, as if walking on saplings!
Now, for as long as he followed the sandy terrain were his footsteps
Very conspicuous, all of them, easily, there in the dust, but
Soon indecipherable grew the tracks of himself and the cattle
340 When they had crossed a large tract of the sand and were walking on
firm ground.
Nevertheless did a mortal remark him as straight toward Pylos

Hermes was driving a herd of my cattle, the kind with broad foreheads.
When he had penned them in peace and confounded the left and the
   right side
Of his way back by his dodges, he lay in his wickerwork cradle
Feigning the stillness of night, under dusk, in the murk of the cavern.   345
Nor could a sharp-sighted eagle have spotted him, even as, very
Frequently rubbing his eyes with his fists, he was brewing deception.
So he immediately answered, unprompted, indifferently saying,
'I've not seen anything, nor have I heard the report of another.
Therefore, I cannot inform you or win the reward of informers.'"   350
When he'd concluded his evidence, Phoebus Apollo was seated.
Hermes, however, pronounced a rebuttal before the immortals,
Pointing at Cronus's son, Zeus, the Director of all of the gods, "Zeus,
Father, to you I shall publicly tell the whole truth of the matter:
I am extremely veracious and do not know how to embroider.   355
He came to our house this morning, the sun having recently risen,
Seeking his shambling cattle, he said, and produced not a blessed
Eyewitness nor any god who would testify on his behalf, but
Ordered me under duress and constraint to provide information,
Threatening often to cast me down into great Tartarus forthwith,   360
Since he possesses the delicate flower of honest young manhood:
I was, however, born yesterday—something he very well knows—nor
Can I be said to resemble a rustler of cattle, a he-man!
You will believe me: you boast that you are my affectionate father!
I haven't driven his cattle to *my* house (so may I be happy!),   365
Nor—I declare this with certainty—did I step over the threshold.
Helios I hold in honor, the other divinities also,
You in affection, but this one in dread and aversion. You know your-
Self, I am innocent! Mighty and binding the oath I shall utter:
No! by these nobly proportionate porticoes of the immortals!   370
Someday I shall be revenged for this pitiless interrogation,
Strong though he is. And do you, Father Zeus, now give aid to the
   younger."

So, with a wink, said the slayer of Argus conceived on Cyllene,
Holding his clothes on his forearm, unwilling to cast off his cover.
375 Almighty Zeus laughed aloud when he saw how his mischievous infant
Well and expertly denied that he knew anything about cattle.
Both of his sons he commanded to search with unanimous purpose,
Hermes the Guide to go first on condition of blameless intent to
Point out the place where he'd actually hidden the powerful cattle.
380 Cronus's successor then nodded and glorious Hermes obeyed him;
Very persuasive the purpose of Zeus, who emblazons the aegis!
Both of the beautiful children of Zeus hurried on till they came to
Pylos, constructed on sand, and the ford of the Alpheus river.
Further, they came to the meadows and entered the high-raftered cow
    barn
385 Where the possessions of Phoebus Apollo were cherished at nighttime.
There, while his brother was gone to the rear of the cavern of rock to
Drive forth the powerful kine into daylight, the offspring of Leto,
Glancing aside, as it happened, remarked and then recognized some
    hides
Stretched on a rock in the sun, and immediately questioning Hermes,
390 "How did you manage to do it? to skin these two heifers? a newborn
Baby, an infant, as you are, however deceitful and cunning?
Much I admire your strength when I think of it! There is no need, O
Offspring of Maia conceived on Cyllene, for you to grow bigger!"
While he was talking, he plaited strong bands round the wrists of the
    child, of
395 Willow, which fell to the ground and took root at his feet quickly, till it
Twisted inextricably by itself and grew over the cattle
Utterly, at the command of delinquent young Hermes. Apollo
Marveled as soon as he saw it. And then the strong slayer of Argus
Furtively gazed at the ground, as his glances were flashing with fire,
400 Eagerly wishing to hide. But the offspring of glorious Leto,
Stern though he was, was as easily tamed as his brother could wish.
Holding the lyre on his left with a plectrum, accordingly Hermes

Tuned it, and under his touch it resounded miraculously, so
Phoebus Apollo was moved to delight and to laughter, because the
Lovable note of the marvelous music went straight to his midriff   405
As he was listening, and a sweet yearning laid hold of his senses.
Bolder, the offspring of Maia then stood on the left hand of Phoebus,
Beautifully strumming the lyre; and thus to the zither's shrill music
Presently chanted a prelude; and lovely the sound that ensued. He
Told of the undying gods and the universe when it was darkest,   410
How they first came into being and each was allotted his portion.
First in the course of his song did he celebrate Memory, mother
Of the nine Muses, the goddess to whom Maia's son was devoted.
Next in seniority other immortals the glorious son of
Zeus celebrated, relating how each of them came into being.   415
Everything fell into place in his narrative sung to the zither
Held in the crook of his arm. But incurable passion inflamed the
Breast of Apollo, who spoke, using words that went straight to their
    target,
"Killer of cattle, resourceful, laborious feasting companion,
What you have improvised easily equals in worth fifty cattle!   420
Now I suppose that our differences will be tranquilly settled.
Tell me, however, this much, very devious offspring of Maia,
Has it—this marvelous, magic performance—been yours since your
    birth, or
Did some immortal or someone of men, who are born but to perish
Give you this glorious gift and inculcate the art of inspired song?   425
Wonderful, truly, the music, unuttered till now, that I hear now,
Which I declare that no mortal has ever before comprehended,
Nor have the undying gods who inhabit the halls of Olympus,
None except you, O you rascally by-blow of Zeus and of Maia!
What is this art? this new Muse that assuages impossible sorrows?   430
What is this practice? For, truly, it offers us three things together,
Happiness, sexual love, and the pleasures of sleep, for the choosing.
I am a fan of the muses, the Muses that dwell on Olympus,

Who are concerned with the dance and the glorious course of the art
    song,
435 Also the flourishing choir and the heart-thrilling thunder of
    woodwinds.
Yet, of the clever performances common at parties of young men,
None has affected me thus in my feelings the same way that this does.
Son of our Father, I marvel how fetchingly you play the zither.
Now that, albeit so little, you know such distinguished devices,
440 Sit, my dear fellow, and hearken a bit to a word from your elders.
You shall have certain renown in the company of the immortals,
You and your mother; and this I'll infallibly promise in public:
Yes, by my cherrywood shaft, I shall make a respectable sponsor
Of you among the immortals and render you fortunate also.
445 Glorious gifts shall I give you and, finally, never deceive you."
Hermes replied to Apollo and cleverly worded his answer.
"Warden, you question me closely. However, I do not resent the
Magnitude of your intruding upon my professional secrets.
This very day you shall know them. I want to be on the best terms with
450 You, in intention as well as expression. You know about all things
Surely, intuitively, inasmuch as among the immortals,
Son of our father, you sit in preeminence, goodness, and power.
Zeus, the great counselor, loves you: it's perfectly right that he should
    do:
Often he's given you glorious gifts, and they say at his bidding
455 You comprehend all the honors and oracles of the immortals,
Even the secrets of Zeus, distant guardian, all his pronouncements:
Knowledge which I have so recently learned, you are richly endowed
    with!
Now it is only a matter of mastering what you've a mind to,
Seeing your humor is eagerly set upon playing the zither:
460 Sing and strike up an accompaniment on the instrument, go on,
Take it from me, and prepare yourself glory and merriment. My dear,

Do me the honor and, holding your clear-voiced companion-in-arms,
    chant
Beautifully, since it knows how to discourse in an eloquent fashion.
Fearlessly take it along hitherto when you go to a dinner
Party or dance (so attractive), or to a respectable revel,   465
Merry by night and by day. For whoever, instructed in wit and
Craftsmanship, asks of it anything, him with articulate voice it
Teaches all manner of things that delight the intelligence. It is
Easily played with a minimum of far from difficult practice,
Seeming to shun all unpleasant exertion. However, the first who   470
Questions it violently in his ignorance, him it repays at
Once with a jangling discord, and then it plays tunelessly off key.
Since it is merely a matter of mastering what you've a mind to,
This I shall make you a gift of, O glorious son of our Father.
I shall go pasture our cattle who graze at discretion in grassland,   475
On the horse-nourishing prairies and meadows high up in the
    mountains.
There, when the cows have been put to the bulls, they shall bear in
    abundance,
Bull calves and heifers alike; therefore, little necessity is there,
Phoebus, although you're a capitalist, to get frightfully angry."
When he had finished, he proffered the lyre, which Apollo accepted,   480
Pledging his glittering whip in exchange for the gift and ordaining
Hermes his herdsman; delighted, the infant of Maia accepted.
Leto's all-glorious son, the Far Guardian, lordly Apollo,
Taking the lyre on his arm, with a plectrum accordingly tuned it;
Under his touch it resounded miraculously, and he chanted.   485
Not long thereafter, the cattle returned to their god-given meadow.
Back to excessively snowy Olympus Zeus's beautiful children
Hurried, amusing themselves with the lyre. The counselor, Zeus, was
Glad for them both, and he brought them together in friendship, for
    Hermes

490 Steadily held in affection the son of Latona (and does now),
When he had given the lyre, his desirable emblem, in pledge to
Phoebus, the long-distance archer, who played it as he had been taught
  to,
Held in the crook of his arm. For himself, he discovered the secret
Of an alternative science. He fashioned the note of the pan pipes,
495 Audible at a great distance. But Phoebus addressed him then, saying,
"I am afraid, my dear boy, that a pathfinder, devious witted,
Clever as you, will make off with both zither and bent bow together,
Seeing that you have a charter from Zeus to establish transactions,
Trade, and exchange among men over all the exceedingly fertile
500 Earth. But if you are so bold as to swear the great oath of the gods by
Nodding your head, or upon the all-powerful waters of Styx, then
You would do all, to my mind, that is friendly and gives satisfaction."
Then did the infant of Maia, inclining his head, undertake that
Never would he pilfer anything owned by the long-distance archer,
505 Nor would he ever go anywhere near his strong house. And Apollo,
Son of Latona, agreed to his friendship and to the condition
That he would never hold anyone dearer among the immortals,
Whether a god or a mortal descendant of Zeus. "And a perfect
Symbol thereof I shall make for immortals and everyone else, both
510 Trustworthy to my desire and honorable. For hereafter
I shall give you a most beautiful scepter, for wealth and for riches,
Golden and branching in three, which will guard you from harm and
  accomplish
All of the precepts concerning both virtuous words and good actions
Which I declare I have learned from our father's oracular edict.
515 As for the power of prophecy that you have mentioned, dear fellow,
It is not lawful for you, although nurtured of heaven, to learn it,
Nor for another immortal. The mind of our father alone knows
This, wherewith I am entrusted, agreeing and swearing a potent
Oath, that no other but me of the gods, who're engendered forever,
520 Shall comprehend the considered and confident counsels of Zeus. So

Do not, dear brother endowed with the scepter of gold, do not ask me
Ever to utter the secrets our far-sighted father considers.
One among men I may injure; another I'll cover with kindness,
Leading in circles the multiple tribes of despicable mortals.
But he who follows the sound of my voice and the flights of portentous   525
Birds shall have joy of my utterance, and I shall never deceive him.
He who, believing in vainly loquacious and meaningless omens,
Wants to discover our prophecy, contrary to our intention,
And to know more than the gods, who exist for eternity, I say
His is a vain expedition—although I accept what he offers.   530
Then I shall tell you another thing, child of respectable Maia,
Son of our father, who carries the shield made of goatskin, light-
    fingered
Genius: there are mysterious ladies (by birth they are sisters),
Maidens rejoicing in wings, of a swiftness, a reverend trio
Who have their heads thickly sprinkled with powder, the whitest of   535
    barley.
Under a fold on the slopes of Parnassus do they make their dwelling,
Teachers, apart, of a different art of foretelling the future,[10]
Which I once practiced myself as a child when I followed my cattle,
Arts of which Father, however, was never exactly approving.
Out of their hive, here and there, to and fro, how they flit on occasion!   540
Feeding on honeycomb, seeing to everything to be accomplished.
When they have eaten their fill of fresh honey, divinely inspired,
Then are they willing and eager with forethought to utter the truth, but
If they are ever deprived of the deities' saccharine diet,
Swirling about in a swarm, they'll tell nothing but falsehood thereafter.   545
These, then, I give unto you, and do you by your accurate questions
Please first your own inclinations. And if you instruct any mortal,
Often, if he is in luck, will he hearken unto your pronouncements.

10. Divination by pebbles, as suggested by the name—Thriae—of these mysterious,
beelike beings.

Take them, dear infant of Maia, and also the rambling cattle;
550 See that you tend them, the horses and also the hard-working donkeys."
Thus, over cruel-eyed lions and boars with bicuspids of silver,
Over the dogs and the sheep that extensive earth nourishes, over
All of the beasts of the field, he made glorious Hermes the master.
And he appointed him plenipotentiary messenger unto
555 Hades, who, although implacable, shall give him not the least honor.
Thus was the infant of Maia befriended by lordly Apollo
With every kindness, to all of which Zeus added grace in abundance.
So he associates freely with all, both immortal and mortal,
To their advantage, a little; but under the darkness of night he
560 Constantly leads to perdition the nations of men, born to perish.
Herewith, farewell, mighty masculine infant of Zeus and of Maia!
Presently I shall remember another about you and sing it.

V. TO APHRODITE

Muse, will you narrate the doings of her who has plenty of gold, the   1
Cyprian queen, Aphrodite, who rouses the gods to desire?
She has completely subdued every kind of man born but to perish,
She is the mistress of airborne birds and of every creature
That the dry land is a nurse to and deep waters breed in abundance;   5
All of them share a concern in the deeds of the garlanded goddess.
Yet is she powerless over three minds, to persuade or mislead them:
Owl-eyed Athena the virginal daughter of shield-bearing Zeus, to
Whom the affairs of her opulent sister convey little pleasure;
Battles to her are delightful and all of the work of the warlord,   10
Combats and fights and the shrewd preparation of brilliant
     achievements.
She was the first who instructed the craftsmen of earth to construct
     the
Scythian car and the various chariots made out of metal;
She it was also who taught soft-complexioned young maidens domestic   15
Splendid achievements and planted their knowledge in every bosom.
Nor has the goddess of smiles, Aphrodite, by lust ever conquered
Artemis, her of the arrows of gold, the loud-hallowing huntress:
Dear to her rather are archery, snaring of game in the mountains,
Music of lyres, also dances, and piercingly shrill ululation;
Shadowy thickets and groves are her home, and the city of just men.   20
Nor do the Cyprian's doings appeal to one reverend spinster,
Hestia, eldest begotten of Cronus whose counsels were crooked,

Youngest, again,[11] the last born at the instance of shield-bearing Zeus, a
Ladylike goddess Apollo once courted and also Poseidon.
25　She was extremely unwilling, however, and sternly refused them,
Swearing a terrible oath, and an oath which has never been broken,
Laying her hands on the head of her brother who carries the aegis,
To this effect, to continue a virgin the rest of her days, this
Queen among goddesses, whom father Zeus, in lieu of her marriage,
30　Granted fair honor: she sits in the midst of the house and obtains the
Fat of the feast as her portion. Revered in the temples of all gods,
She is considered by men universally eldest of all gods.
These are the spirits that love is unable to sway or deceive, but
None of the others! Not one of the rest has escaped Aphrodite,
35　Whether a blessed immortal or man that is born but to perish.
She has seduced the intelligence of the delighter in thunder,
Even great Zeus, who is greatest, and greatest his portion of worship;
Utterly has she beguiled his impervious wits as she pleases,
Easily making him mingle with women who're born but to perish,
40　Lightly abandoning Hera, his sister and also his consort,
Who is by far of all undying goddesses best in appearance
And the most honored, for Cronus whose counsel is crooked, begot her
Once, and her mother was Rhea, and Zeus, who knows thoughts that
　　are deathless,
Made her his reverend wife, with her knowledge of serious matters.
45　But in the heart of the temptress herself he implanted desire to
Lie with a man born to perish, in order that presently she might
Not be without all experience of the embrace of a mortal,
Never might make it her boast in the presence of all the immortals,
Pleasantly laughing and frequently dimpled in smiles, Aphrodite,
50　How she had mingled the gods with the daughters of men born to
　　perish,
Who to the undying gods then bore sons who were destined to perish,

11. First swallowed and last disgorged by Cronus?

Mating the goddesses also with men who are born but to perish.
Zeus, for the love of Anchises, implanted sweet yearning in her heart,
Who, in the heights of the mountains, on Ida, abounding in fountains,
Pastured his cattle—in form and physique he was like an immortal.   55
Once she laid eyes on Anchises, the lover of smiles, Aphrodite,
Loved him, and longing forthwith laid a vehement hold on her feelings.
Flying to Cyprus, she landed at Paphos and entered her fragrant
Temple, for there are her precinct and incense-odiferous altar.
After she entered the temple, she shut its splendiferous portals.   60
There her attendants, the Graces, first bathed her and rubbed her with
     fragrant
Oil of ambrosia, which they anoint all the goddesses with who
Ever endure, an ambrosial sweetness with which she was scented.
When she had fitted her pretty apparel upon her completely,
Neatly adorning her body with gold, Aphrodite went smiling   65
Straight toward Troy, and she left all of Cyprus sweet-smelling behind her.
High in the air among clouds she pursued her impetuous journey.
Coming to Ida, abounding in fountains, the mother of wildlife,
Over the mountain she went to the hut of the shepherd directly.
Whereupon terrible-eyed cat-a-mountains and sinister gray wolves,   70
Leopards and bears, very swift and incessant pursuers of roe deer,
Followed her, fawning; this sight, when she saw it, delighted her humor.
Into the bosoms of all, she injected desire, so that they
Coupled together promiscuously in the shadowy hollows.
Then she proceeded until she arrived at a comfortable steading;   75
There she discovered Anchises alone in the shelter, abandoned
By his companions: a hero, his beauty derived from the gods. The
Others were all away putting the cattle to grass in the pastures.
He, in their absence, was left by himself in the hut and amused his
Solitude pacing around as he thrillingly played on the zither.   80
Standing in front of Anchises, the daughter of Zeus, Aphrodite,
Made herself look like an unmarried girl in appearance and stature,
Lest he should be badly frightened to recognize her when he saw her.

When he beheld her, Anchises was filled with amazement and wondered
85   At her appearance and stature and also her shimmering raiment,
Since she was wearing a mantle outshining in brightness the firelight,
Torques that were twisted in spirals, and glittering flower-shaped
     earrings;
Necklaces lay on her delicate neck, of surpassing refinement,
Beautiful, golden, and cunningly fashioned; a luster of moonlight
90   Shone round her delicate body, which was a great wonder to witness.
Longing laid hold on Anchises, who spoke to her something as follows,
"Greetings, milady, whichever you are of the blessed who come here
Visiting: Artemis, Leto, perhaps Aphrodite the golden?
Themis of aristocratic descent, or Athena the gray-eyed?
95   Or are you one of the Graces come here on a visit? the Graces,
Who are companions of all of the gods and are reckoned immortal?
One of those nymphs are you, rather, frequenters of beautiful thickets?
Or are you one of the nymphs that inhabit this beautiful mountain,
Maidens who dwell at the sources of rivers and haunt grassy meadows?
100 I shall construct you an altar upon a conspicuous station,
High on a lookout, and there I shall offer you beautiful, holy
Sacrifice at every season. Do you of your own inclination
Kindly see that I become a preeminent man of the Trojans.
Grant me hereafter a flourishing progeny, but for myself, give
105 Me a long life and a happy, continual sight of the sunshine:
Fortunate may I, among my own people, attain age's threshold!"
So did the daughter of Zeus, Aphrodite, return him an answer:
"Noblest of men who are born on the face of the earth, wise Anchises,
I am no goddess: so why do you liken me to the immortals?
110 For I was born but to die, and the mother who bore me was mortal.
Otreus is father's name, and a famous one—maybe you've heard it?
He is the overlord over all Phrygia, fortified strongly.
Both of our languages, yours and my own, can I comprehend clearly,
Seeing my nanny at home was a Trojan, who nursed me and raised me,
115 Taking me from my dear mother when I was no more than a baby.

That is the reason that I understand very well your own language.
Just now, the slayer of Argus, the wand bearer, Hermes, removed me
Out of the choir of the loud-crying huntress, whose arrows are golden,
Artemis, where, many maidens of prosperous family and nymphs, we
Sported together, a numerous crowd that revolved in a circle.   120
Out of their midst the destroyer of Argus, the wand bearer, snatched me,
Bearing me off over mortal mankind's manifold manufactures,
Over the wasteland as well, the un-built-up, where ravening wildlife
Wanders at will, the carnivorous haunters of shadowy hollows—
Till I supposed that I never again should set foot on the good earth,   125
Giver of life, while he said I was called to the couch of Anchises,
To be your titular wife and to bear you all-glorious children.
When he had spoken and shown me the way, the strong slayer of Argus
Straightway departed again to the company of the immortals,
And I have come on to you, as the strength of necessity moved me.   130
But on my knees I beseech you, by Zeus and your virtuous parents,
(For you are such that no wicked or basely born folk could have bred
      you),
Take me unbroken, unskilled as I am in all sexual science,
And introduce me at once to your father and right-thinking mother
And to your brethren begotten and bred of identical parents.
I shall not prove an unsuitable in-law for them, but a likely.   135
Send off a messenger quickly to Phrygia, home of swift horses,
Telling my father and mother, who grieve for my absence, the story.
Soon they will send you much gold and sufficient attire closely woven;
Do you accept it in turn as a plentiful, glorious dowry.   140
When this is done, you may ready the feast and desirable wedding,
Honorable in the sight of mankind and the gods, who are deathless."
When she had finished, the goddess implanted sweet lust in his bosom.
Love laid a hold on Anchises, and these were the words that he uttered,
"If you indeed are a mortal, and mortal the mother that bore you,   145
And if your father is Otreus as you assert—a renowned name—
And if you come here because the immortal conductor has brought you—

Hermes—and are to be called my espoused for ever and ever,
No one, not one of the gods or of men, who are born but to perish,
150 Here shall restrain me until I have lain down with you as a lover
Instantly, now, though the accurate archer Apollo himself should
Launch from his bow made of silver his terrible death-dealing arrows!
I should be perfectly willing, O woman in Goddess's likeness,
Once I have mounted your couch, to descend to the dwelling of Hades!"
155 Saying these words, he took hold of her hand. Wreathed in smiles,
 Aphrodite
Crept to the comfortable bed that already was spread for its master,
Strewn with luxurious cloaks, and on top of that heaped up with furs
 like
Bearskins and pelts that belonged to the deep-throated lions he
 slaughtered
High in the mountains; she went, although turning aside at each step
 and
160 Casting her beautiful eyes, as if hesitant, bashfully downward.
When they had clambered together upon the well-carpentered
 bedstead,
First he removed all the glittering ornaments decking her body,
Brooches and necklaces, spiral-shaped bracelets and flowerlike earrings,
Then he proceeded to loosen her girdle and shimmering garments;
165 Taking them off her, he laid them aside on an armchair of silver.
Thus did Anchises, fulfilling the will of the gods and of heaven,
Lie with an immortal goddess, unconscious of what he was doing.
When it was time for the herdsmen to turn once again to their shelter,
Bringing their cattle and corpulent sheep from the flowering meadows,
170 Then Aphrodite poured over Anchises a slumber delicious,
Deep and refreshing, while she was resuming her beautiful clothing.
When she had clad herself well and completely, the glorious goddess
Stood in the hut, and her head touched the handsomely carpentered
 roof-beam.
Heavenly loveliness shone from her transfigured countenance such as

Characterizes the face of the garlanded queen of Cythera,   175
As she awoke him from sleep, and she uttered his name and addressed
    him:
"Rise, son of Dardanus! Why are you sleeping a sleep without waking?
Tell me, do I now appear in your eyes at all similar to the
Woman that first I appeared to be when you beheld me and knew me?"
Such was her speech. In his sleep, he immediately heard and awakened.   180
But when he saw the corsage and the beautiful eyes of the goddess,
Terrified then, he averted his gaze, turned aside from her presence;
Hiding his beautiful face in the folds of the blanket again, he
Spoke as a supplicant, using swift words that flew straight to their
    target,
"Goddess, the moment I saw you the first time, I knew that you were a   185
Goddess, but you did not tell me the truth. On my knees, I beseech you,
By Father Zeus, he who wields the tempestuous buckler of goatskin,
Do not condemn me to dwell among men for the rest of my lifetime
Impotent! Pity my manhood; for never a vigorous man is
He any more in his lifetime who lies with an immortal goddess."   190
Then did the daughter of Zeus, Aphrodite, return him an answer.
"Most highly honored of men, who are born but to perish, Anchises,
Be of good cheer, do not entertain fear overmuch in your conscience,
Since there is nothing to fear, nothing evil to suffer from me or
Any among the immortals; indeed, you are dear to the blessed,   195
And you will get a dear son who will rule as the lord of the Trojans,
Children in turn will be bred of his children without intermission.
He shall be known as Aeneas, or 'Shamefast,' because of the shame and
Anguish I felt at the time I was laid on the bed of a mortal.
Nearest of all of mankind, who are born but to perish, were ever   200
Those of your race, by the way, to the gods in appearance and stature.
Notably, golden-haired Ganymede: Zeus, the dispenser of counsel,
Grabbed him because of his beauty and brought him to join the
    immortals,
Where, in the palace of Zeus, he is wine steward, serving the gods, a

205 Wonderful thing to behold! and respected by all the immortals,
As from a beaker of gold he dispenses the ruby-red nectar.
But inconsolable sorrow laid hold of the heart of old Tros, for
Where the miraculous whirlwind had rapt his dear son, he did not
    know.
Therefore, he groaned and lamented incessantly every day till
210 Zeus had pity upon him and gave him as Ganymede's ransom
High-stepping horses, the kind that are used to convey the immortals.
When he had given him these as a gift all his own to possess, the
Guide, the Destroyer of Argus, at Zeus's command told him each and
Every thing: how his son, like the gods, would be deathless and ageless.
215 And when the father of Ganymede, Tros, had heard all Zeus's message,
Never again did he groan or lament, but was glad in his heart, and
Gaily he used to go riding abroad with his wind-footed horses.
Similarly did the goddess whose armchair is golden, Aurora,[12]
Kidnap your kinsman Tithonus, who looked very like the immortals.
220 For him, she went to the black-clouded son and successor of Cronus
Begging this boon, that Tithonus be deathless and might live forever;
Zeus indicated assent with a nod, and her wish was thus granted.
Silly Aurora! That lady did not recollect enough sense to
Ask also youth for Tithonus and that he should shed dreadful old age.
225 For, just as long as extremely admired and desirable youth held,
He was a source of delight to Aurora, the goddess of morning,
With whom he dwelt by the river that runs round the edge of the world.
    But
When the first silvery hairs had begun to appear in the locks that
Fell from his beautiful head and to sprout from his aristocratic
230 Chin, then the lady Aurora avoided his bed altogether,
Although she cherished him still in her halls, where she long
    entertained him

12. Dawn.

On an ambrosial diet, while giving him beautiful clothing.
But when the weight of detestable age altogether oppressed him,
So that he neither could move with his limbs nor could even sit upright,
This was the plan that seemed best in the goddess Aurora's opinion: 235
Laying him up in his chamber, she bolted the radiant portals;
There his unquenchable voice babbles endlessly though there's no
    motion
Left of the sort that there once used to be in his sinuous members.
Such would I rather not see you, Anchises, among the immortals,
Being thus deathless and living, or rather surviving, forever!   240
Only if just as you are in appearance, and with the same figure,
You might endure and were called, dear Anchises, my consort,
Then would anxiety never envelope my powerful feelings.
Now, as it is, very soon universal old age will enfold you,
Age that is pitiless, waiting in ambush beside every human,   245
Wearisome age, much lamented; the gods that are deathless detest it.
Yes, my disgrace will be great, and eternal, and uninterrupted,
All on account of yourself, in the eyes of the gods, the immortals,
Who before now were afraid of my converse as well as the wiles by
Which I have mated the gods one and all unto women of mortal   250
Kind, inasmuch as my intellect influenced every one. But
Now will my tongue lack the strength to relate the whole story in detail
To the immortals, of how I have erred in infatuate folly
Wretchedly: no laughing matter! I must have been out of my mind to
Sleep with a mortal, whose baby I'm carrying under my girdle.   255
Him, when he first sees the light of the sun, will his nurses attend to,
Deep-bosomed oreads, nymphs who inhabit this high, holy mountain,
Nymphs who by nature are numbered with neither immortals nor
    mortals.
Long do they live on the earth, and ambrosial food is their diet,
And they perform in the beautiful dance with the other immortals;   260
With them Silenoi and Hermes, the sharp-sighted slayer of Argus,

Mingle in love in delicious recesses of underground caverns.
When first they come into being, there spring simultaneous with them
On human-nourishing earth lofty firs and tall, toplofty oak trees
265 Clothed in luxuriant foliage, flourishing up in the mountains
Beautifully; steeply they stand; mortals call them the natural precincts
Of the immortals, and nobody cuts them with axes of iron.
But when their doom is upon them, and death, which is everyone's
portion,
Creeps up upon them, their beautiful leaves on the ground lie all
withered,
270 Sadly the bark all about them decays, and their branches are fallen.
Then do the souls of the nymph and the tree quit the daylight together.
These are the nymphs who, adopting my baby, will nurse him among
them,
And when he first has attained the desirable era of childhood,
Here will the goddesses bring him to you, to present you your offspring.
275 Now—and in order that I may discover the whole of my purpose—
I shall return to you round the fifth year and will bring the boy with me.
When you behold him at first, like a flourishing stalk, with your own
eyes,
You will rejoice at the sight, for he will be exceedingly godlike.
Then you conduct him immediately unto Ilion's[13] windswept
280 City. If anyone asks you, of men, who are born but to perish,
Who was the mother who carried this son of yours under her girdle,
Do you remember to tell them a story, as I shall instruct you:
'He is the offspring, they say, of some nymph with a face like a flower,
Such as inhabit this mountain whose shoulders are mantled with forest.'
285 But, should you speak out and boast of the fact, in your ignorant folly,
That you have mingled in love with a handsomely garlanded goddess,
Zeus in his anger will strike you with blackening thunder and lightning.

13. Troy.

Everything now has been told you; consider it well in your own heart;
Stay! do not mention my name, but respect the immortals' displeasure."
When she had spoken, the goddess arose on the breezes of heaven.   290
Hail and farewell to you, goddess, comptroller of civilized Cyprus!
Having begun with a hymn about you, I shall turn to another.

VI. TO APHRODITE

1   Reverend, beautiful, decked out in garlands of gold, Aphrodite
    Shall be my song, who obtained as her portion the fortified cities
    All over Cyprus enisled in the sea, where the watery west wind's
    Impulse had ferried her over the swell of the bellowing sea on
5   Pillows of billowing foam. There the Hours, with their golden tiaras,
    Welcomed her graciously, wrapping ambrosial garments about her,
    Crowning her heavenly head with a beautiful, handsomely fashioned
    Garland of gold; through the lobes of her ears, which were pierced, they
        depended
    Flowers of copper alloy and of valuable gold, and upon her
10 Delicate neck and her silvery bosom the Hours adorned her
    With golden necklaces just like the ones that the golden-tiaraed
    Hours themselves are adorned with whenever they go to attend the
    Lovely dance of the gods or to visit the house of their father.
    When they had put all her ornaments on her, they brought Aphrodite
15 To the immortals, who, having beheld her, at once made her welcome,
    Taking her into their arms; every one of the gods importuned her
    To be his own wedded wife and accompany him to his dwelling,
    Marveling at the appearance of violet-crowned Cytherea.
    Greetings, sweet ogler, lascivious spirit of kindness, dear goddess,
20 Grant me in this competition the victory; harness my song, and
    Presently I shall remember another about you and sing it.

VII. TO DIONYSUS

Now of the god Dionysus, respectable Semele's offspring,   1
I shall recall the appearance upon the unharvested seashore,
High on a prominent headland: he looked like a young adolescent
In the first flower of youth, with his beautiful coal-colored ringlets
Shaken in curls all about him and wearing a purple-dyed mantle   5
Over his powerful shoulders—when presently, out of the distance,
Over a wine-colored sea and aboard a well-outfitted vessel
Swiftly, Tyrsenian pirates approached—evil fortune their loadstone.
As they beheld Dionysus, they nodded unto one another,
Leapt from their ship to the shore, where they quickly laid hold of the   10
   god and
Set him erect in their vessel, with hearty complacence because they
Thought him the scion of kings that are nurtured by heaven. They tried
   to
Cruelly bind him; however, the bonds would not hold him. The fibers
Started apart from his hands and his feet, and he just sat there smiling
Out of his sea-colored eyes. Then the pilot, who had recognized him,   15
Called out at once to his comrades, "You fools! Do you know who this
   mighty
God is whom you, having seized, are attempting to bind? Why, not even
Our sturdy ship is sufficiently strongly constructed to bear Him.
Say, is He Zeus? or perhaps He's the silver-bowed archer Apollo?
Maybe Poseidon? Because He most certainly doesn't resemble   20
Men who must perish, but rather the gods who inhabit Olympus.
Come, let us set Him at liberty on the mysterious mainland

Instantly; do not attempt to lay hands on Him, lest, in his anger,
He should raise troublesome winds and invoke a most terrible tempest."
25 So said the pilot. The captain returned a detestable answer:
"Fool! Do you notice which way the wind's blowing? Why, then, put out
    canvas,
Laying on all of the rigging on board. As for him, he's our business,
Men's business. Sooner or later, I hope he'll reach Egypt or Cyprus,
Maybe the back of the north wind—or maybe beyond! In the
    meantime
30 He shall provide us at last with the names of his friends and relations,
Telling us all they possess. A divinity handed him to us."
Therewith, he put up the mast and he hoisted the sail of the vessel.
Breezes inflated the canvas and tightened the rigging about it.
Soon there began to appear to the pirates incredible marvels.
35 Wine, to begin with, ran bubbling all over the deck of the black ship,
Wine as delicious to taste as to smell; an ambrosial odor
Rose. And amazement laid hold of the crew one and all when they saw
    this.
Then all at once on the top of the sail there extended a grapevine
Hither and thither, with plentiful bunches of grapes dangling from it.
40 Ivy encircled the mast, shiny, black, with luxuriant blossoms;
Fruit ripened pleasantly on it; a garland festooned every oarlock.
Finally, after the sailors had seen this, they called to the pilot
Quickly to put in to shore. But in front of their eyes Dionysus
Turned himself into a lion, right there in the ship. On the foredeck,
45 Mightily roaring, he stood—something dreadful! And meanwhile,
    amidships,
Great Dionysus had cunningly fashioned a bear with a shaggy
Mane: thus displaying his emblems. The bear stood erect on her hind
    legs,
Ravening; forward, the lion stood glowering horribly, fiercely,
Whereby the pirates were terrified aft, where they gathered about the
50 Right-thinking pilot all stricken with terror, till, all of a sudden,

He—Dionysus, the lion—sprang onto the skipper and gripped him.
All of the men, when they saw this, evading a horrible fate, then
Leapt from the vessel in unison into the glittering salt sea,
Where they were turned into dolphins. However, the god in his mercy
Held back the pilot and made him exceedingly happy, and told him,   55
"Be of good cheer, my dear fellow, for you have delighted my humor.
I really am Dionysus, the Thunderer. Semele bore me,
Semele, Cadmus's daughter, in sexual union with great Zeus."
Hail to you, offspring of lovely-faced Semele! There is no way by
Which anybody who once has forgot you may order the sweet ode.   60

VIII. TO ARES

1 Ares—exceedingly puissant, oppressor of chariots, golden
   Helmeted, savior of garrisons, powerful-spirited, strong-armed
   Shield-bearer clad in bronze armor, unwearied Olympian bulwark,
   Strength of the javelin, father of Victory, happy in battle,
5 Ally of Justice and tyrant of enemies, leader of just men,
   Sceptered commander of masculine virtue, revolving your fire-bright
   Orb through the midst of the sevenfold path of the planets in aether
   Where, incandescent, your coursers maintain you above the third
       orbit—
   Listen, defender of humans and giver of flourishing youth, let
10 Shine a propitious ray from above on the course of our lifetime,
   Grant us your martial strength, to the end that I may be enabled
   Once and for all to remove wretched cowardice far from my person,
   Also to conquer within me the treacherous urge of my spirit;
   Help me as well to control the sharp passionate temper provoking
15 Me to embark upon blood-chilling mayhem, and give me the courage,
   Blest, to remain in the comfortable legal prescriptions of peacetime,
   Thereby avoiding the conflict of foes and a violent ending.

IX. TO ARTEMIS

Muse, sing a hymn about Artemis, sister of Phoebus, the Archer,   1
Maidenly strewer of barbs who was nursed at the breast with Apollo.
When she has furnished her steeds at the deep reedy stream of the
    Meles,
Swiftly through Smyrna she urges her chariot, gilded all over,
Unto the vineyards of Claros; the silvery bowman, Apollo,   5
Sits there, awaiting his sister, the accurate strewer of arrows.
This is my greeting to you and all goddesses, lyrical greetings!
You I sing first and, moreover, from you I commence to make music.
Having begun with a hymn about you, I shall turn to another.

X. TO APHRODITE

1   Now I shall sing the Cytherean, born upon Cyprus, who gives to
     Mortals her gifts, which are kind; and upon her desirable face there
     Always are smiles, and the bloom of desire is effulgent upon it.
     Hail to you, guardian goddess of pleasant Salamis, the queen of
5   Cyprus, enisled in the sea! Yours the gift of desirable song, and
     I shall remember yourself and a ballad about you and sing it.

XI. TO ATHENA

Pallas Athena, the city's protector, I shall begin singing: 1
Dreadful is she, her concern is with Ares, polemics and war work,
Sackings of cities concern her and bellicose shouting and battles.
Yet it is she that protects all the populace going and coming.
Hail to you, goddess, please grant me good luck and felicitous fortune.   5

XII. TO HERA

1   Hera I sing on her throne made of gold, her whom Rhea gave birth to,
     Deathless, a queen and a goddess possessed of superior beauty,
     Sister and consort of Zeus, who contends with the voice of the thunder,
     Reverend, whom all the blessed that live upon lofty Olympus
5   Hold in like honor and awe as great Zeus, whose delight is in thunder.

XIII. TO DEMETER

August Demeter, the goddess with beautiful hair I commence to   1
Sing, her exceedingly beautiful daughter, Persephone, also.
Greetings, great goddess, preserve this our city, begin the cantata.

XIV. TO THE MOTHER OF THE GODS

1   Muse with a thrilling delivery, daughter of Zeus, the almighty,
    Sing me a hymn to the mother of all of the gods and of humans,
    Her whom the racket of rattles and drums and the thunder of
        woodwinds
    Equally please with the howling of wolves and of cruel-eyed pumas,
5   Also the echoing mountains as well as the forested valleys.
    Thus I salute you and all of the goddesses with you in music.

XV. TO HERACLES, THE LIONHEARTED

Heracles, scion of Zeus, shall I sing, who is vastly the best man   1
Born upon earth. Him Alcmene gave birth to in Thebes, with its
    handsome
Orchestras, when she had lain with the black-clouded offspring of
    Cronus.
Over ineffable earth long ago and across the wide sea when
Wandering at the behest of the lord Eurystheus, his master,   5
Heracles did many violent deeds and endured very many.
Now in the beautiful home of the gods upon snowy Olympus,
Happy he dwells and delighted. For wife he has trim-ankled Hebe.
Hail, Son of Zeus, Master, grant us your virtue and worldly success too.

XVI. TO ASCLEPIUS

1   I am inditing this song for Asclepius, healer of sickness,
    Son of Apollo. Asclepius noble Coronis conceived and
    Bore on the Dotian flatland—Coronis, king Phlegyas's daughter.
    He is the joy of mankind, the assuager of painful diseases.
5   Thus I salute you, O Lord. In my poem I utter my prayer.

XVII. TO THE DIOSCUROI

Muse with the silvery voice, sing the ballad of Castor and Pollux,   1
Grandsons of king Tyndareus; Olympian Zeus was their father.
Under the peaks of Taygetus, ladylike Leda produced them,
Having submitted in secret to Zeus, the controller of storm clouds.
Greetings, Tyndaridae, horsemen that mount on the swiftest of horses.   5

XVIII. TO HERMES

1   Hermes I sing, who was born on Cyllene, the slayer of Argus,
     Governor over Cyllene and pastoral Arcady also,
     Light-fingered messenger of the immortals, whom Maia gave birth to,
     Maia, the daughter of Atlas, who mingled in liking with great Zeus.
5   Modestly, then, she avoided the company of the immortals,
     Kept to her shadowy cave, where the scion of Cronus resorted
     Under the cover of night to consort with the pretty-haired nymph,
        when
     Sleep had deliciously gripped, so he hoped, white-armed Hera, his
        consort,
     All unbeknownst to the deathless and men, who are born but to perish.
10   This is my greeting to you, son of Zeus and respectable Maia.
     Having begun with yourself, I shall turn to another cantata.
     Hail to the guide and the giver of grace and of benefits, Hermes!

XIX. TO PAN

Tell me now, Muse, all about him, the favorite gotten of Hermes,   1
Goat-footed, doubly horned, and a lover of noise. Through the
    meadows
Crowded with thickets, he wanders together with high-stepping
    nymphs, who
Tread on the tops of the rocks that the goats had avoided, invoking
Pan as the pastoral god with the glorious ringlets, the squalid   5
Deity who has obtained as his portion all snow-covered ridges;
Mountaintops also and ways which are rocky belong to his worship.
Hither and thither he wanders where undergrowth bushes are thickset,
Strongly attracted, perhaps, at one moment, by soft-flowing streamlets,
Picking his way on another occasion through towering rock-cliffs,   10
Climbing the loftiest summit of all to keep watch on his flocks from.
Often he hunts on the foothills, successfully slaying much wildlife,
Peering about him acutely. But only at evening as he
Sometimes returns from the chase, does he play on his pipes a seductive
Melody: none there is who can compete in melodious sounds, not   15
Even the bird that in flowery springtime concealed among leaves most
Pours forth her plaint and laments in her song while her voice is like
    honey.
Then do the nymphs of the mountain accompany Pan with soprano
Voices and, nimble of foot, by the side of a spring of dark water,
Wander and chant; meanwhile, Echo makes moan round the tops of the   20
    mountains.
This side or that of the choir, or intruding himself in their midst, the

Deity nimbly performs with quick footwork, while wearing the spotted
Skin of the lynx on his back, entertaining his heart with the nymphs'
　　shrill
Song in a comfortable meadow where crocus and hyacinth blossom
25　Fragrantly, mingled together innumerable in the tall grass.
Sagas they sing of the gods that are blessed—and of lofty Olympus—
Such as of Hermes, his light-fingered excellency, above all the
Others, and how he became the swift messenger of the immortals,
Furthermore, how he first came to Arcadia, flowing with fountains,
30　Mother of flocks, where his precinct is set as the Lord of Cyllene.
There it was he, though a god, used to shepherd his crinkly-coated
Sheep for his master, a mortal, because of the languishing lust that
Visited him and increased, to make love to the daughter of Dryops.
When he'd accomplished their genial union, she bore at her home a
35　Favorite son unto Hermes, albeit bizarre in appearance,
Hoofed and twin-horned like a kid, very noisy and lustily laughing.
When she beheld him, his mother was frightened and leapt to her feet
　　and
Fled from the sight of his rough, bearded face, and abandoned her baby.
Light-fingered Hermes adopted the infant immediately, and
40　Superabundantly glad was the deity's heart as he held him.
Swiftly he went to the seats of the deathless, conveying the baby
Cozily wrapped in the skins of some hares that frequented the
　　mountain.
Setting him down beside Zeus then, in front of the other immortals,
Hermes exhibited him as his son, and at heart the immortals
45　All were delighted, especially so Dionysus, or Bacchus.
Pan he was called, which means "all," thus, because he gave pleasure to
　　all hearts.
Hail to you, Lord. It is thus I propitiate Pan in my hymnal;
I shall remember a different song about you and rehearse it.

XX. TO HEPHAESTUS

Sing, sweet, articulate Muse, of Hephaestus, the famous inventor,   1
Who, with the goddess Athena, the gray-eyed, instructed mankind in
Glorious crafts upon earth, even men who were heretofore used to
Living in caves in the mountainside, for all the world just like wild
    beasts.
Nowadays, thanks to Hephaestus, the famous technician, they know the   5
Arts and the crafts and are able in peace to conduct their existence,
Perfectly, all the year round, as they please, and secure in their own
    homes.
Show us your favor, Hephaestus; prosperity grant us with virtue!

XXI. TO APOLLO

1   Phoebus, the swan sings of you with clear note and with musical wing-
         beats
     As it alights with a bound on the bank of the eddying river
     Peneus; you does the rhapsode whose diction is pleasant remember
     Always to sing first and last as he handles his resonant lyre.
5   This is my greeting to you, O my Lord; I implore you in music.

XXII. TO POSEIDON

It is my purpose to sing about holy and mighty Poseidon,   1
Mover and shaker of earth, the unharvested sea-bottom also,
Maritime ruler of Helicon and the extensive Aegean.
Earth-quaker, twofold the roles that the gods have assigned you in
    worship,
Both as a breaker of horses as well as the savior of vessels.   5
Greetings, upholder of earth with the sea-colored locks, O Poseidon,
Blissful divinity, please be kindhearted and succor all sailors.

XXIII. TO ZEUS

1   Zeus I shall sing: of the gods he is best, he is also the greatest.
Wide is his vision. He governs and brings everything to fulfillment,
Whispering words unto Themis, who sits inclining toward him.
Favor us, scion of Cronus, all-seeing, most honored, and greatest!

XXIV. TO HESTIA

Hestia, who as a housekeeper serves in the sacrosanct home of   1
Lordly Apollo, the long-distance archer, at excellent Pytho,
Endlessly out of the hair of your head the slick oil is exuded.
Come to this house and with spirit take heart and come unto this
    dwelling.
Come with the counselor, Zeus, and grant grace, too, to this   5
    composition.

XXV. TO THE MUSES AND APOLLO

1   I shall begin with the Muses, Apollo, and Zeus, in that order,
     For on account of the Muses and Phoebus, the long-distance archer,
     Singers exist upon earth, also men who perform on the zither,
     Whereas our kings are from Zeus. He is happy whomever the Muses
5   Love and befriend; from his lips, in a stream, issues speech, of a
          sweetness!
     Greetings, you children of Zeus, see you crown my performance with
          honor,
     And I shall surely remember yourselves and a different music.

XXVI. TO DIONYSUS

I am beginning a song of deep-voiced Dionysus, his forehead   1
Circled with ivy, Zeus's glorious son and respectable Maia's,
Whom certain elegant nymphs took to nurse from his masterful father,
Welcoming him to their laps, where they sedulously entertained him
There in the crannies of Nysa. He waxed, at the will of his father,   5
Great in their sweet-smelling cave, being numbered among the
    immortals.
But when the goddesses had educated this subject of many
Hymns, he began to prefer to frequent the well-forested hollows,
Decked out in laurel and ivy. His nurses the nymphs used to follow
Him as their leader; the uproar filled all the intractable forest.   10
So it is that I salute you, abundant in grapes, Dionysus.
Grant that we may come again every year to this season rejoicing,
Season by season returning for year after year in the future.

XXVII. TO ARTEMIS

1   Artemis, clamorous huntress, I celebrate: gilt are her arrows,
Terrible virgin assaulter of stags with a volley of arrows,
Sister, indeed, of Apollo, whose ritual saber is gilded;
She, through the shadowy mountains and over the high, windy
     headlands,
5   Takes her delight in the chase as she stretches her parcel-gilt bow and
Launches her accurate shots; then the towering crests of the lofty
Mountaintops tremble, the forest resounds, and the underbrush echoes
Dreadfully to the complaint of the beasts, and the earth even shivers,
As does the fish-swarming deep. But the goddess is very stouthearted;
10 Every which way that she turns she destroys generations of wildlife.
Yet when this shooter of beasts with a shower of barbs has enjoyed her
Sport and has gladdened her heart, then she loosens her neatly curved
     bow and
Goes to the spacious abode of her only and dearly loved brother,
Phoebus Apollo, and enters the opulent province of Delphi,
15 Where she arranges the beautiful dance of the Muses and Graces.
There, having hung up her double-bent bow on a hook with her arrows,
Artemis, wearing her elegant bodily ornaments, leads and
Starts off the dance, and the rest, pouring forth their ambrosial voices,
Sing about Leto with beautiful ankles, how she bore these children,
20 Best of immortals by far, both in counsel and other achievements.
Hail to you, children of Zeus and of Leto the beautifully coiffed. Now
I shall remember you both, and another about you, and sing it.

XXVIII. TO ATHENA

Pallas Athena, illustrious goddess, I sing to begin with.   1
Gray are her eyes, and her wisdom is great, but her heart is unyielding;
Terrible virgin, austere and courageous protector of cities,
Tritogeneia, whom Zeus by himself in his wisdom engendered
Out of his worshipful head. She came wearing the armor of battle,   5
Golden and glaring all over, and awe seized on all the immortals
When they beheld her. In front of her father, who carries the aegis,
Issued the goddess impetuously from his heavenly forehead,
Shaking a sharp-pointed javelin. Mighty Olympus went reeling   10
Dreadfully under the impact of gray-eyed Athena, and round it
Earth gave a horrible groan, and the depths of the sea were excited,
Seething with purplish waves, and the salt water swell was suspended
Suddenly. Meanwhile, Hyperion's glorious son, having stayed his
Swift-footed horses, remained where he was for a while, until virgin   15
Pallas Athena removed from her immortal shoulders her godlike
Armor. Then Zeus, the deviser of counsel, was heartily gladdened.
Here is my greeting to you, child of Zeus, who is armed with the aegis,
And I shall surely remember yourself and another song also.

XXIX. TO HESTIA

1   Hestia, you have obtained in the high-ceilinged homes of all parties,
Whether the immortal gods' or humans', who go upon earth, a
Place everlasting, respect, veneration, and honor, and worship.
Yours is a beautiful privilege also, and honor; without you
5   There are no banquets for mortals, for nobody pours the libation
At the beginning, of honey-sweet wine unto Hestia, first and
Last. With the slayer of Argus, the offspring of Zeus and of Maia,
Messenger unto the blessed, whose wand is of gold, handsome giver,
Live in your beautiful dwellings, endeared in your hearts to each other.
10   Hermes, propitious, aid us, along with august and beloved
Hestia. Both of you, knowing of men, who are born upon earth, the
Noble achievements, support them with intellect, also with vigor!
Hail to you, Cronus's daughter, and you with the golden rod, Hermes!
I shall remember you both and an alternate hymn on this subject.

XXX. TO EARTH, MOTHER OF ALL

Earth, who is mother of all, shall I sing on her noble foundation;   1
Eldest is she and she feeds every thing that exists in the world, all
Those that inhabit the glorious surface of earth and the deep sea,
Plus those that fly in the air—they are fed, every one, from your
    bounty!
By you are excellent children and fruitfulness brought to perfection,   5
Lady; there lie in your hands both the giving of life and the taking,
Where mortal men are concerned. He is happy whom you in your
    humor
Willingly honor, for everything then will be his in abundance.
For him the vegetable furrow is fertile, and throughout his pastures
Livestock are thriving; his home overflows with prosperity likewise.   10
Men such as this, by good order, in cities with beautiful women,
Dominate, plentiful plenty and wealth their appropriate portion.
Theirs are the sons that exult in a mirth that is constantly newborn,
Maidenly daughters who cheerfully mingle in flower-decked choirs,
Skip and disport themselves over the delicate pastoral flowers.   15
Such are the folk that you honor, dread Goddess and generous spirit.
Hail to the Mother of Gods and the consort of star-spangled Heaven!
Give in return for my song kindly livelihood suiting my temper,
And I shall try to remember another about you and sing it.

XXXI. TO HELIOS

1   Daughter of Zeus, O Calliope, Muse, undertake now to hymn the
Radiant sun, whom the wide-beaming, ox-eyed one, Euryphaessa[14]
Bore to her brother the offspring of Earth and of star-spangled Heaven.
Know that Hyperion wedded with glorious Euryphaessa,
5   His very sister, who bore to her husband three beautiful children:
Dawn with her rose-colored arms, and the Moon with her glorious
     tresses,
And the unwearying Sun, who is certainly like the immortals,
He who illuminates men who must die and the gods who are deathless
As he proceeds with his steeds, and he terribly glares with his eyes from
10 Under his helmet of gold, meanwhile luminous beams all about him
Brilliantly coruscate. Down from his temples the luminous cheek-
     guards
Over his head are protecting his gracious, far-visible visage.
On him there glows—on his body—a beautiful, delicate garment
Stirred by the breath of the wind. And the horses below him are
     stallions.
15 When he has halted his golden-yoked chariot there, and the horses,
Marvelously he conducts their career through the sky to the ocean.
Hail to you, Lord, in your mercy assure me a hearty subsistence.
Having departed from you I shall praise the articulate human
Race—demigods in whose deeds you, the gods, have instructed us
     mortals.

14. "Widely beaming."

XXXII. TO SELENE

Maidenly daughters of Cronian Zeus who are experts in music,   1
Muses, rehearse in sweet phrases a song of the volatile Moon, whose
Brightness embraces the earth when her light, as displayed in the
    heavens,
Shines from her immortal brow, whence in plenty embellishment rises
Under her splendid effulgence. The lusterless atmosphere lightens,   5
Catching the gold from her crown, and her beams are as lucid as
    daylight.
Thus, when the brilliant Selene, done bathing her beautiful body
Dipped in the ocean, and donning her garments that gleam from afar,
Laying her yoke on the necks of her shining, high-spirited coursers,
Drives on her horses with beautiful manes in impetuous speed, at   10
Evening, at the full moon, her magnificent orbit is filled, and
As she increases, her beams reach their brightest perfection in heaven,
Making the Moon a dependable token and sign unto mortals.
With her the scion of Cronus once mingled in friendship and slumber;
She, growing pregnant, gave birth unto Pandia, who is a maiden   15
With an exceptional beauty of form even for an immortal.
Hail to you, goddess and queen with white arms, brightly shining
    Selene!
Favorable, beautifully coiffed. Having started with you, I shall sing the
Praises of men who are semidivine, whom the Muses' attendants
Celebrate—poets with admirable tongues—as they tell their   20
    achievements.

XXXIII. TO THE DIOSCUROI

1   Muses with quick-rolling eyes, will you tell us about the twin sons of
    Zeus, the Tyndaridae, glorious children of fair-ankled Leda,
    Castor, a tamer of horses, and physically fit Polydeuces.
    Under the peak of the summit of mighty Taygetus, Leda
5   Bore these two boys to be saviors of those who are dwellers on earth and
    Also of swift-sailing ships, when tempestuous gales rush and bluster
    Wintrily over the pitiless deep. Then the persons on shipboard,
    Praying, invoke to their aid the Dioscuroi, sons of great Zeus, with
    White sacrificial lambs; they proceed to the deck of the forward
10 Bow, but a powerful wind and a wave of the sea overwhelm the
    Prow and submerge it—when suddenly these twin gods make their
        appearance,
    Darting impetuous down through the air upon whistling pinions;
    Instantly they have arrested the gusts of the troublesome winds and
    Leveled the turbulent swells on the face of the white frothy salt sea.
15 Beautiful omens to sailors are these of deliverance; seeing
    Them, they are gladdened and cease for a while from all tiresome effort.
    Greetings, Tyndaridae, riders upon the most rapid of horses!
    I will remember a song of yourselves and another performance!

THE BATTLE OF THE
FROGS AND THE MICE

I shall begin by beseeching the chorus of Helicon: Muses,   1
Visit my innermost heart for the sake of the narrative poem
I have put down in original form on my lap on these tablets.
"Strife beyond measure, lamentable battle, the work of the War God"
Fain would I bring to the hearing of every articulate person,   5
And in what manner the frogs and the mice, to see who were the better,
Went out as if emulating the feats of chthonian giants.
Such is the tale among men. And it had its beginning as follows.
Once did a mouse that was thirsty, escaped from the threatening
    polecat,
Put forth his delicate muzzle beside a large body of water,   10
Taking delight in the honey-sweet taste of the drink. There espied him
One whose great joy was the swamp, many voiced, and he uttered this
    question:
"Stranger, who are you? and whence do you hail to this shore? and who
    was it,
Tell me, begat you? Now tell me the truth of it all and don't let me
Think you are lying; for if I consider you worthy of friendship,   15
I shall invite you to *my* house and give many generous presents.
I am his Majesty Swellcheek that throughout the length of the swamp
    am
Ruler and Lord of the Frogs and am held in perpetual honor.
Peleus,[1] known as Old Muddy, the father that bred me, he wed with

---

1. The name of Achilles' father, emphasizing the burlesque epic character.

20 Hydromedusa, or 'Water Princess,' by the steep Eridanus.
You, I can see, are both handsome and brave, a Superior Person
Doubtless, a king by your scepter, and also a fighter in battle.
Come then, as quickly as possible your genealogy tell me."
Crumbgrubber answered him shortly and something or other as
    follows,

25 "Why do you seek to inquire my people? For they are well known to
Everyone, mortals and gods and the winged celestial creatures.
I am called Crumbgrubber, that is my name, and I boast me the son of
Crustcrusher; he was my big-hearted father, and as for my mother,
She was a Licker of Millstones and daughter of King Nibblehambone;

30 And in a cottage she bore me and fed me the following victuals:
Figs, also nuts, and such dainties and eatables of all description.
How would you make me your friend who resemble you nowise in
    nature?
You have your life in the water, but I am accustomed to nibble—
Such is my character—food fit for humans, and nothing escapes me,

35 Neither the thrice-kneaded cake in its elegant circular basket
Nor the flat sesame-cheesecake, for all its elaborate wrapping,
Neither a helping of ham nor the liver in white, fatty tunic,
Neither the fresh-curdled cheese that is pressed from the sweetest of
    whole milk
Nor the delectable honeycake that is desired by the blessèd,

40 None of those things that are fashioned by cooks for the banquets of
    humans
When they make ready their pots using spices of every description.
Radishes, cabbages, pumpkins, however, I never do nibble.
Nor do I browse among salads and vegetables, fennel or parsley;
These are your fodder or grub, who inhabit these lacustrine regions."

45 Thereto did Swellcheek reply with a smile in the following phrases,
    "Stranger, you boast overmuch of your belly![2] But there are among us

---

2. A reference to Hesiod, *Theogony*, 25: "merely bellies."

Manifold wonderful things in the marsh and on land to admire,
Seeing how heaven has given us frogs an amphibious lifestyle,
Leaping about on dry land and immersing our bodies in water,
And in alternative elements dwelling in different houses.   50
If you would learn of such matters as these, it's exceedingly easy:
Hop on my back and hold on to me tightly or else you might perish;
Thus, you will come to my home and arrive there securely in gladness."
When he had spoken, he offered his back, and as quickly the other
Mounted him, grasping his delicate neck in the lightest of clutches.   55
First, he was cheerful enough as he looked on the neighboring
     moorings
And took delight in the swimming of Swellcheek; but when he was wet
     by
Purplish surges and billows, beginning to weep in abundance,
Blaming his useless repentance, he started to pluck at his fur, and
Pulled in his paws up tight under his belly, his stomach within him   60
Fluttered because of his novel condition; he wished to reach dry land.
Dreadfully groaning aloud in the throes of his tingling terror,
First, he extended his tail like an oar that he dragged in the water,
Fervently praying the gods he might presently reach terra firma.
But as the darkening water drops dashed him, he begged all the more   65
     for
Succor and hopelessly uttered the following words and discoursed thus:
"Was it like this that the Bull on his back bore the Burden of Love when
Over the billowy surge he abducted Europa to Crete?[3] No,
Not as this frog ferries me on his back to his home, like a sailor,
Lifting his ivory hide just above the immaculate water."   70
Suddenly, what should appear but a water snake, horrible sight to
Both of them! raising his neck straight and upright and out of the water.
When he caught sight of it, Swellcheek submerged, never giving a
     thought to

3. In the form of a bull, Zeus carried off the nymph Europa to Crete.

How he was bound to abandon the other to utter destruction.
75 Down to the depths of the pond did he sink as he warded off black
    doom.
Mouse like a castaway fell over backward, right into the water,
Wringing his paws like the victim he was, and pathetically squeaking.
Time and again he would sink under water and time and again he
Surfaced still kicking, and yet he could not get away from his death, the
80 Weight of his fur saturated with water was great and it dragged him
Down. As he perished, he uttered these words at the very last minute:
"Swellcheek, you won't get away with your treachery! What a
    performance—
Throwing me off of your body as if from a rock, like a shipwreck!
Wretch! You could not get the better of me any way upon dry land,
85 Whether in versatile wrestling or running a race. You misled me,
Cast me away in the water, but God has an eye for injustice;
Someday you'll pay for your crime; no escaping an army of field mice!"
When he had said the foregoing, he gave up the ghost in the water.
Lickplatter saw him, while seated upon the salubrious bank, and
90 Set up a terrible plaint as he ran to report to the mice, whom,
When they had learned of his fate, an extreme indignation came over,
Every one. They instructed their heralds to summon a meeting
Just before dawn at the mansion of Crustcrusher, who was the noble
Father of unhappy Crumbgrubber, who was at present extended
95 Flat on his back in the pond, an exanimate body: and no more
Near to the shore, wretched creature, he floated, but out in the middle
Deep. So they gathered in haste before dawn, and the first to stand up
    was
Crustcrusher, very indignant because of his son, and he said so:
"Friends, although I have, alone of the mice, suffered manifold wrongs,
    yet
100 This has been done to you all as a specimen, simply, of evil.
Certainly I am unfortunate, seeing I've lost all three children;
First was the one who was kidnapped and killed by the criminal ferret,

Worst of our enemies, that is, who caught him outside of the mouse
    hole.
Pitiless men were the death of another again, whom they brought to
Doom by original means: they invented a snare made of wood—they   105
Call it a mousetrap—it spells the destruction of mice altogether.
Ah, but the third was the darling of me and his reverend mother!
This one did Swellcheek abduct and asphyxiate under the water.
Come, therefore, put on your armor and let us go forward against the
Foe, when we've decked out our bodies with cunningly wrought martial   110
    harness."
Such were the phrases with which he persuaded them all to get armed,
    and
Ares, whose business is warfare, equipped them, moreover, with
    helmets.
First did they fasten the greaves on, whereby they protected their
    shinbones,
Greaves that were made of green beans that they split into two equal
    portions,
Chewing them out overnight, on their feet, as they stood to their labor.   115
Breastplates they had that were made out of hide that was stretched over
    wattles,
Hide that they cleverly had manufactured by flaying a ferret.
Shields were the broken-off bases of oil lamps; a spear was a pointed,
Well-tempered needle of unalloyed bronze, a creation of Ares,
As were the helmets they set on their temples, the shell of a peanut.   120
Thus were the mice up in arms, and the frogs, when they learned of the
    matter,
Rose from the water as one and then, coming together in one place,
Swiftly collected a council of war—which is ever an evil.
While they were holding an enquiry what all the noise was about and
What was the issue, a herald approached with the wand of his office.   125
This was the scion of valiant Cheesegrater, Envoy of Saucepan,
Bringing the sad declaration of war, and his words were as follows:

"Frogs, I am sent unto you by the mice and with this admonition,
Namely, to tell you to gird on your armor for warfare and battle.
130 For they have seen in the water one Crumbgrubber, him whom your
  monarch,
Swellcheek, undid, in fact, murdered. They bid you come out and do
  battle,
Such of you frogs who do boast yourselves men and pretend to some
  valor."
Thus and in so many words he proclaimed. His impeccable discourse
Came to the ears of the arrogant frogs and excited their rancor;
135 As they were blaming him anyway, Swellcheek arose and addressed
  them:
"Comrades, I tell you, I neither did murder this mouse nor was witness
Of his demise. He was drowned, by all evidence, while he was playing
Down by the pond, imitating the swimming of frogs—and these
  wretches
Now put the blame upon me, who am guiltless! But let us invent a
140 Plan whereby we may undo all these mice, who think they are so clever!
And I shall tell you, moreover, what seems to me best as procedure.
Fitting our bodies in armor, let's take up our stand all together,
Right on the critical lip of the precipice, where there's a drop-off.
Then, when the mice make an infantry charge and are almost upon us,
145 Grab every one by the topknot the mouse that opposes him nearest,
Casting them, helmets and all, in the pond—they'll go straight to the
  bottom.
Thus, when we've drowned in the water our enemies, who are no
  swimmers,
Cheerfully we shall erect a memorial Mouse to their slaughter."
Saying as much, he persuaded them all to get into their armor.
150 So they enveloped their sinewy shins in the leaves of the mallow,
Corsets they had that were made of the finest and greenest of beet
  leaves,

Shields they had beautifully fashioned themselves from the leaves of the
    cabbage.
Each had a long, pointed reed of his own as a javelin, and they
Covered their heads, for protection, with spiral-shaped, delicate snail
    shells.
Then they combined like a bulwark and stood on the heights of the   155
    bank, and,
Shaking their spears, they were filled, every one, with a bellicose spirit.

Zeus it was summoned the gods to their places in star-spangled heaven,
Showing them first the assembly of war and the warriors, mighty,
Many, and grand, who were carrying, each of them, dangerous
    weapons—
Like, he pretended, an army of centaurs or, even, of giants.   160
Laughing delightedly, Zeus put a question to all the immortals,
Which they would favor, the frogs or the mice? and addressing Athena,
"Daughter," he said, "you would go to the aid of the mice, I imagine?
Seeing the way that they always are skipping about in your temple,
Fed on the fat from the sacrifice, stuffed with all manner of dainties."   165
So said the scion of Cronus; in answer, his daughter Athena:
"Father, it's never the mice in distress that I'd come to the aid of,
Seeing it's these very mice who have done me such manifold mischief,
Damaging garlands and ruining oil lamps because of the fuel.
One thing they've done in particular bothers me more than all others—   170
Look! they have chewed a big hole in this robe which I wove with such
    labor,
Knitting the delicate weft with a web that was rather substantial—
Now it is all full of holes, and the mender is after me, too, and
Charges me interest, which is an insult to any immortal!
Since, having spun out of need, I have nothing to pay his investment.   175
Yet I am not of a mind to support the amphibia, either.
They are not really reliable. Once, I returned from a battle

Early, but while I was stricken with weariness, they wouldn't let me
Sleep, though I wanted to badly, for all of the noise they were making—
180 Not even doze for a little! I swear, I lay utterly sleepless,
Head aching horribly, until the cockerel shouted Good Morning.
No, let us prudently cease, fellow gods, all assistance to either
Party, lest one of our number get hurt by a sharp-tempered weapon.
These are such infighters, even, indeed, if a god come against them.
185 But, let us, rather, amuse ourselves, watching the conflict from heaven."
This was Athena's advice, and the several gods were persuaded
By it, and all of them gathered together again in the one place.

Thereupon, herald-mosquitoes equipped with astonishing trumpets
Sounded the terrible challenge to battle, and forthwith, from heaven
190 Zeus shortly thundered, the signal for war, which is always an evil.
First, lofty Croaker inflicted a sword wound upon manly Licker,
Getting him right in the gut, through the belly, in forward engagement.
Forward he fell on the ground, where he got his soft fur pretty dusty!
Falling to earth with a thud and a rattle and clatter of armor.
195 Holedweller next threw a javelin straight at the son of Old Muddy,
Smiting him right in the breast with his stout spear, and as he collapsed,
black
Death laid a hold of him, so that his spirit flew out of his mouth. Then
Beety struck Saucepan Ambassador straight through the heart and thus
killed him,
Cheesegrater, there on the bank, did he utterly extirpate also.
200 Reedy, beholding the Carver of Hambones, was horribly frightened;
Running away, he abandoned his shield and jumped into the water.
Brewer in turn to immaculate Mudhusband forthwith fell victim,
Struck on the head with a boulder, so that which had been in his
forehead
Oozed from his nostrils, commingled with blood, and the earth was
bespattered.

Then was immaculate Mudhusband slain in his turn by one Lickdish,   205
Rushing upon him with weapon in hand; darkness covered his eyes, too.
Leeky, beholding this, though he was already dead, grabbed his ankle;
Dragging him into the lake, he proceeded to asphyxiate him.
Crumbgrubber, who was avenging his friends who had died in the
    struggle,
Struck this same Leeky before he could get himself up onto dry   210
    land.
Forward he fell, and his soul went its way to the dwelling of Hades.
Seeing this sight, Lord Mountcabbage, directing a handful of mud at
Him, so anointed his muzzle he blinded him almost completely.
Crumbgrubber then in his anger did pick up a stone in his mighty
Fist—an immense one that lay on the ground like a load on the   215
    plowland—
With this he belted Mountcabbage one under the kneecap. His whole
    right
Shin being shattered, Mountcabbage collapsed on his back in the dust.
    But
Croaker the scion of Croaker took vengeance and, falling upon him
Once again, struck him a blow in the midst of the belly. The entire
Shaft of the sharp-pointed reed disappeared in him so that the other's   220
Bowels poured out on the ground as he pulled back the spear with his
    stout hand.
Holedweller, when he beheld this, was limping away from the battle
There on the height by the river and really got frightfully rattled;
Quickly he jumped in a ditch and avoided thus utter destruction.
Crustcrusher then dealt a blow on the toe unto villainous Swellcheek—   225
Finally, he had emerged from the pond and was terribly bothered;
Leeky, who saw him prostrated and yet only partially breathing,
Pressed through the front of the fray and delivered his sharp-pointed
    spear. His
Shield wasn't shattered; however, the point of the spear was arrested.

230 Godly Oregano, something in action resembling Ares,
Walloped him on his immaculate helm, which was made of four
kettles—
He who, alone of the frogs, was superior in the ensemble—
Then made a sally, but seeing one coming, he did not await the
Powerful hero, but forthwith submerged in the depths of the frogs'
pond.

235 Now there was one of the mice quite exceptional, Great Helping-
Snatcher,
Favorite son of Old Scratch, the impeccable bakery brigand;
When he got home he had summoned his son to take part in the battle.
He it was threatened to utterly ravage the race of all frogkind.
Breaking a nutshell in two down the ridge of the middle, he fitted

240 Both of the hollowed-out halves on his paws as a sort of protection.
All of the frogs, who were rapidly frightened, ran down to the pond, and
Surely he would have accomplished his boast, for his might was
impressive,
Had it not come to the critical notice of Him who is Father
Both of the gods and of humans, who pitied the frogs as they perished.

245 Shaking his head in amazement, he uttered the following statement.
"Tut-tut! It's wonderful what a To-Do I behold with my own eyes!
Down by the pond Helping-Snatcher is sowing no trivial panic
Where he is paying the frogs back rapaciously. Quickly as may be,
Let us send Pallas, who raises the war whoop, or possibly Ares.

250 *They* will restrain him from fighting, no matter how mighty this
mouse is!"
So said the scion of Cronus, but Hera spoke up with an answer:
"Neither the strength of Athena nor that of redoubtable Ares
Would be enough, son of Cronus, to save all the frogs from destruction.
Come, let us go to their aid, every one—unless you set in motion

255 Your privy weapon, the Wreaker of Wrath and the Slayer of Titans,
With which you slew once that powerful chap Capaneus,
Mighty Enceladus also, all the uncivilized giants.

Set it in motion, involving in ruin whoever is boldest."
These were her words. The successor of Cronus let fly with a lightning
Bolt, but first thundered and shook the foundations of mighty   260
    Olympus.
Then came the thunderbolt, afterward, Zeus's most terrible weapon:
Whirled in a circle, it flew from the hand of the Lord of Creation,
Frightening all of the creatures he visited thus with his thunder.
Yet did the army of mice not desist; rather, more did they hope to
Utterly vanquish the race of the warrior frogs, and had done so   265
Had not the scion of Cronus had pity on them from Olympus,
So that he sent to immediate aid of the frogs certain allies.
Suddenly, out came these creatures with steel on their backs and with
    crooked
Claws, walking sideways, all twisty and scissor-mouthed; pottery-hided,
Bony, and broad in the beam were these beasts, and with glistening   270
    shoulders,
Bandy of leg and distended of limb, with their eyes in their bosoms.
Feet they had eight of, and tops they had two of, but hands they had
    none of—
"Crabs" are they called; and they nipped off the tails of the mice in their
    pincers,
Also their feet and their hands, whereas spears were but blunted upon
    them.
Fearful are mice, and they feared them and kept their positions no   275
    longer.
Turning to flight every one, they escaped. And, behold! it was sunset:
Done was the War of One Day and complete, and the end was
    accomplished.

INDEX

25091243R00135

Made in the USA
Lexington, KY
12 August 2013